SCARED TO DEATH...

Do It

Anyway!

By

Brian Beneduce

&

Steven R. Porter

Scared to Death...
Do It Anyway!
By
Brian Beneduce
& Steven R. Porter

Scared to Death... Do It Anyway!

Copyright © 2016 Brian Beneduce. Produced and printed by Stillwater River Publications. All rights reserved. Written and produced in the United States of America. This book may not be reproduced or sold in any form without the expressed, written permission of the authors and publisher.

Visit our website at **www.StillwaterPress.com** for more information.
First Stillwater River Publications Edition

Library of Congress Control Number: 2015956405
1 2 3 4 5 6 7 8 9 10
Written by Brian Beneduce & Steven R. Porter
Photographs from the Beneduce Family Collection. Reprinted with permission.
"Anxiety Tree" Original Illustration by Jamie Forgetta
Cover design by Dawn M. Porter.
Published by Stillwater River Publications, Glocester, RI, USA.

Publisher's Cataloging-In-Publication Data
(Prepared by The Donohue Group, Inc.)

Beneduce, Brian.
  Scared to death... do it anyway : one man's journey from debilitating fear to happiness, wealth and success / by Brian Beneduce & Steven R. Porter. -- First Stillwater River Publications edition.

  pages : illustration ; cm

  ISBN: 978-0-692-56970-2
  ISBN: 0-692-56970-7

  1. Beneduce, Brian. 2. Agoraphobia--Patients--Biography. 3. Fear. 4. Self-realization. 5. Success. I. Porter, Steven R. II. Title.

RC552.A44 B46 2015
616.85/2250092   2015956405

DEDICATION

This book is dedicated to Robbie, my best friend and wife, and to Jennifer and Michael, my wonderful children.

Courage is not the absence of fear,
but the learning to act in spite of it.

~ Theodore Roosevelt

TABLE OF CONTENTS

FOREWORD

Nothing splendid has ever been achieved except by those who dare believe that something inside of them was superior to circumstance.

~ Bruce Barton

I never wanted to write this book.

The mere thought of taking on such a project fills me with apprehension. I've never held great confidence in my writing abilities and I have always considered myself to be terrible at spelling and grammar. In fact, back in high school, I barely passed English. But with recent advances in technology, including the development of speech recognition software, it has become possible for me to now convey my thoughts and feelings more naturally, and overcome those old excuses.

But my apprehension runs deeper than just fumbling with basic English syntax and sentence structure. It is rooted in the excruciating act of opening old wounds to bare my soul and present myself as vulnerable in front of all the people who know me -- or until now, who think they know me.

My biggest concern is always my children. When they were younger, I wasn't able to explain that I had overcome so much to be the successful father they looked up to. Perhaps I thought they were too young yet to understand, or maybe I just wasn't ready to tell them. Then later when they were older, discussing my anxiety and panic attacks with them was still a tremendous challenge for me, yet being the amazing kids that they are, they understood, and embraced me. They continue to look to me as a good father, a man of confidence and a man who values physical fitness and strength. And I remain grateful for that.

But now with this book, there is another part of me they will learn about. After long heartfelt talks with my wife, my business partner, and a few other trusted friends, I came to accept that I am in possession of an important story that needs to be told. It's a story of the torment I went through and how it shaped me as a person. And on a very personal level, it's a story that I want my kids to hear and understand.

It's also a story that will help others who have had to deal with severe fear and panic attacks. I have often found myself sitting in board meetings or coaching on baseball fields and been told, "*Oh yeah,.. I know what you mean. I have anxiety and panic attacks, too!*"

Then I laugh to myself. Sure, everyone experiences nervousness and fear sometimes; it's all part of being human. But very few understand how deep and debilitating a true panic and anxiety attack can be. It is my hope that by writing this book, I can help explain that, and help all those people also afflicted with what I used to call "The Thing" by shedding light on not only what it did to me but also on how it shaped the man I have become.

There is a line in the movie *Draft Day* that says, "sometimes the correct path is the tortured one." On some level, I agree. I recognize that there are many people in this world who have been through a lot worse than I, and I truly am thankful for all that I do have. But this book is my story. It is about an overpowering fear of not being able to leave my house. It's a personal look at *agoraphobia* -- a term I didn't learn until I had suffered for years and reached the lowest, darkest point in my life. And it's about a lonely burden I never shared with my loved ones. How could I? I was a role model for health and physical fitness. I was a leader. I was the strong one. I was the tough guy.

So now that all these years have passed, I am ready to tell my story. It is my hope that by reading about my embarrassing, funny, scary, heartbreaking and happiest moments, someone will be helped. And I hope that this won't just help the children, adults, athletes, business professionals and others who struggle with anxiety and panic attacks every day, but it will also help the people who care about and love them, so they will understand them just a little bit better.

And if you are a true sufferer like me, know that I do understand. And I invite you to use my story as a tool to achieve your hopes, dreams and goals -- whatever they may be.

~Brian

1

THE BRIDGE

The soles of my best dress shoes slammed against the deck of the bridge rapid fire, first right then left as fast as I could move them, creating an eerie echo matched only by my heart pounding with fury in my chest.

My hands were clenched in fists so tight my knuckles were turning blue, and my arms pumped franticly like one of the blow molding machines back in our shop. My necktie was stretched back over my shoulder and stood straight out behind me, and the flaps of my suit jacket flailed and fluttered so fast you'd think I was some bird trying to take flight. Hot car exhaust stung my lungs with each inhale, but no matter how uncomfortable, I would not allow it to slow me down.

If I didn't get off this bridge right now, I knew I was going to die.

My eyes had barely closed the night before. Sleep was impossible. I tossed and turned as my wife slept serenely beside me, oblivious to the fact that the strong, proud man who was lying beside her was lost in a swirl of fear. But my anxiety had nothing to do with the critical meeting I was having the next morning with one of the biggest clients a small businessman could ever hope to land; it was about the simple process of just getting there.

I begged myself, *"Please fall asleep. Stop worrying."*

I planned to leave at 5:15 that morning, determined to beat the infamous rush hour traffic that collected along Interstate 95 every morning from southern Connecticut through New York. My destination was just beyond the George Washington Bridge in Secaucus, New Jersey.

"Please, please go to sleep. I know the truck needs work, but it will make it. It's summer, and traffic will be lighter than usual. Just go to sleep."

And here it was now already 1:30 a.m., and I only had a few hours before I had to get up, shower, put on my suit, grab my briefcase and pretend everything was just great. But the "what ifs" kept flying through my mind. What if I hit traffic anyway? What if I lose control of myself or my car and crash into someone? What if I completely lose it this time, my throat closes and I pass out on the road?

"Go to sleep, damn it. You know where every blue hospital sign is located across the entire state of Connecticut. Everything will be fine."

But what if I make it to the meeting, and they want me to speak to more than three or four people? What if I have a panic attack during the meeting? What if I can't think of an excuse? So what if I just call and cancel then? I could just tell them I'm sick... and my wife will believe that, too, since she knows the kind of workaholic I am. I'm always run down.

"Just go to sleep. Rest. You can't put your family and livelihood at risk over something like this."

But... but what if?

I left that morning even earlier than I planned to see how many exits I could pass before the anxiety became so intense that it would force me to get off the interstate at one of those blue hospital signs. Sometimes just getting off the highway for a moment and knowing the hospital was a few seconds away was enough to ease my anxiety level back from a 5 to a 3, help me catch my breath and allow me to re-focus on my day ahead.

As I traveled farther south, I knew traffic would get worse. It always does. Many people who live in southern Connecticut work in Manhattan and get up very early themselves to fight through the awful, chronic congestion of vehicles.

About an hour and a half into my trip I reached the first tollbooth. My anxiety rose temporarily as I know there is no way to get off nor is there any help available once you are stuck in one of those toll lines. But I gritted my teeth and breezed through this toll quickly. So far, so good. Thank God.

I tuned the radio to New York's WFAN knowing they start the daily traffic reports at 6 a.m. I prayed they wouldn't report a stoppage on the George Washington Bridge -- the only logical connection to Secaucus from where I was. So far, so good.

As I passed through the city of Stamford, Connecticut, I started to see red brake lights ahead of me. Traffic was slowing. Farther ahead, I could see thousands of those red lights stretching out for what appeared to be miles. Red lights symbolize stoppage, feeling trapped. Fear. Panic. There is now nowhere to get off the highway, nowhere to get help, and nowhere to hide. I feel my heart start pounding. My anxiety level instantly shoots to 5.

I started to weave in and out of the lanes the best I could to avoid actually stopping my truck. Above me was a huge green highway sign pointing me toward the George Washington Bridge. I forced myself to follow it. Now there really was no turning back.

My anxiety level rose to 6. I held my breath and continue forward as best I could.

WFAN reported that a tractor-trailer had overturned about a mile before the bridge. Great. Cars had now completely stopped. I was sitting on the Bruckner Expressway on an overpass that felt like it was ten thousand feet off the ground. Everyone around me was pissed at the traffic, but I'm way beyond that, I'm crawling out of my skin. My anxiety rose to level 7.

It's now about 6:45 on a warm, muggy July morning, and as the sun rises, so does the air temperature. The engine in my little Toyota pickup only has four cylinders and I can hear it straining and sputtering. I quickly switched off the air conditioning. I cannot let it overheat out here a thousand feet in the air in traffic, with nowhere to go, and only a million frustrated New York commuters available to help me. The suit I wore -- the only suit I owned -- was made from a thick, warm woolen material designed for winter weather, and now I was sweating right through it.

Traffic was barely creeping along, and the lanes were shrinking from six to four to two to one. I realized none of these jerks were going to let me in. My front bumper came within an inch of the car in the lane next to me, and the driver flipped me off. I swore, screamed and flipped him off right back. I needed that human interaction so bad I was willing to get out and fight him, if necessary. The burst of anger was welcome, but unfortunately, provided only temporary relief.

I had now successfully left the Bruckner Expressway and the massive George Washington Bridge ahead remained my final obstacle. I had timed it perfectly. But WFAN now says this accident had caused about a twenty-minute delay. My heart felt as if it's ready to burst from my chest, and I was drenched in sweat. My tie, which I loosened several miles back, felt as if it's re-tightening around my neck on its own. I am desperately trying to simply continue breathing and not pass out. My fists were pounding on the steering wheel. I was rapidly approaching level 8 panic. I've never experienced a 10 and I am terrified of what it would do to me if I did. Would I even survive it?

My truck inched along as I finally reached the foot of the bridge. My throat was closing even more. Trying to pretend everything is fine, I glanced over at the driver in the car next to me and smiled. I must have looked like a complete moron. I could read the expression on the guy's face: "*What the hell is your problem, asshole?*"

I know that the worst part of the bridge is the middle. At that point, there is no going back and nowhere to get off except to plunge over the railing. Now I am so fucking scared I don't know what to do. Every part of my body was shaking. I glanced down at the briefcase on the seat next to me and realized this is the easiest part of my day -- I still have that big meeting at ten. Someone once said that in life, most of success is just showing up. Well, hell, that is my problem right there -- showing up! Halfway over the bridge, I pulled out my meeting notes and started to shuffle through them, trying to concentrate on the words written on the pages and not the bridge. I begged my truck to not overheat. I looked down again at my notes and they look like scribbles. I didn't even recognize the words I was reading.

I remember trying to switch the radio to a music channel, then panicking when I realized that the station didn't offer traffic updates. I started spinning the knobs, momentarily forgetting how a radio works and couldn't find WFAN. I have AM and FM mixed up. I'm eating up time with these ridiculous distractions, and now I discover I'm three quarters of the way over the bridge. Ahead of me the red lights are starting to disappear, traffic is moving along a tad faster. My anxiety level dropped down to 7, then 6, then 5. I'm starting to feel real again. I felt the muscles in my throat ease and reached for a bottle of water. I tried to drink, but I still couldn't swallow, and now I feared I'll choke and drown. I think to myself:

What the hell is wrong with me? Why can't I even drink a damn bottle of water? Why am I going crazy like this?

People who suffer from anxiety and panic attacks feel and see things that others simply do not. There are thousands of bridges they drive over every day that they don't see. But I see them all. People with anxiety and panic attacks notice and feel every obstacle.

As I neared my Secaucus exit, having survived the George Washington Bridge, I began to drive over some other ordinary and anonymous bridge that was about two miles long and spanned one of New Jersey's many crossways below. I suddenly heard something.

"Oh dear God! Please, no! This can't be happening! Not now! No!"

My engine had overheated. The truck had started to slow.

"Please, please, please let me get to the top so I can at least coast down the other side."

It was my worst fear. I was exactly halfway across this bridge, at the very top, and the truck had quit.

I screamed. I started to cry. Though no one could see or hear me. I pounded on the steering wheel. I was petrified. I got out of the truck, leaving it parked in the right travel lane blocking everyone behind me. They all sat on their horns, waved angry fists and cursed me. I was frantic and didn't give a damn -- in fact the human interaction helped -- so I did the only thing I could think of doing.

I started to run.

Dozens of drivers in a confused daze watched me, a 5-foot 10-inch man in a white dress shirt and tie, sprint past them. I was humiliated by what I thought they were thinking of me. But it did not matter. I had no choice.

When I reached the bottom of the bridge, my shirt was saturated with sweat and my trousers were twisted almost sideways. I'm sure the suit's designers never anticipated it would be worn for a mile-long summer sprint. My hair had matted against my forehead and my cheeks were candy apple red. As I hyperventilated, I looked ahead for a refuge -- some kind of oasis -- where I could stop to try to relax and regain my composure. But ahead, there was nothing but a sea of cars, perhaps a thousand of them, and miles of guardrails and grey highway. I scratched at my face in frustration and terror.

Suddenly, one of the cars came to life in a flash of blue spinning lights. It was a police cruiser and it had worked its way to the breakdown lane to ease up alongside me. I could read the concern in the officer's squinting eyes as he peered at me through his open window. I looked like a complete mess. He had to assume I was being chased by some deranged psychopath, a terrorist, or some rabid wild animal. I was so engulfed in fear I could not speak. He spoke first.

"Are you OK, sir?"

A thousand thoughts ricocheted around inside my skull all at once. I was sure the officer could hear my heart pounding, or even see it pulsating beneath my white dress shirt. I could not let him see how upset I was. As the officer emerged from his car, I noticed the fingers of his right hand were slowly wrapping around the handle of his service revolver. I realized he could not possibly know what he was walking into.

"Everything is fine. Thank you," I lied.

"Then why are you running?"

"Oh... it's because of my pickup truck.... It broke down on top of the bridge... I was on my way to get help... maybe a tow." I tried frantically to catch my breath and sound intelligent, but every word I managed to utter was a struggle.

I assume he thought I was sick, because he kept asking if I was sure I was OK.

Let me say one thing here... there is one phrase you should never say to anyone suffering a severe anxiety and panic attack, and that is, "*Are you OK.*" It is an indication that the person notices and acknowledges that there is something terribly wrong, and it drives the anxiety up to astronomical levels. "*Relax, you'll be OK,*" is another. If I could relax, would I be acting like this? It makes the thoughts in your head swirl until you think you are going insane.

The stone-faced officer acted like he didn't quite believe me, sighed, then waved me into the back seat of his patrol car.

For the briefest of moments, I felt liberated. Help was here. Thank God. Perhaps I had found that temporary oasis in a place that intimidates most people, the backseat of a New Jersey State Trooper's squad car, that I could use to right myself. But sadly, this relief would be temporary.

Because at that moment, the officer uttered a sentence I would remember for the rest of my life.

"You need to stay with your vehicle until a tow truck can take you off the turnpike."

A rush of pure, hot adrenaline swept back through my body. I felt my red cheeks go pale. My throat closed again. I couldn't breathe -- it was a feeling of pure dread. I believed I was going to die. He was taking me back to the top of the bridge. Puzzled, he stared at me through his rearview mirror.

"Are you sure you are alright?"

"I'm just light-headed... from all the running... that's all... I'll be fine... in a few minutes." Then I lied again and told him I had the flu.

"If you're sick, why didn't you stay home?" he asked.

"I just started my own business and I have this very important meeting with one of my first, big customers... in Secaucus."

"Well then, you'd better clean yourself up. You look like shit."

If he didn't have a gun, I would have told him to go screw.

I have the highest respect and admiration for the police, and this officer was no exception. He was young, tall, steel-jawed and in perfect physical shape, obviously a guy who took his job seriously and worked out a lot. How could a fellow tough guy like me explain that I was weak, that I didn't know what was wrong with me, that I was so afraid of being on that bridge that I was running away so I wouldn't jump to my death?

The patrol car was pointing in the wrong direction, so it needed to leave the bridge, take an exit, U-turn, then head back over in the other direction, U-turn again, then drop me at my truck. It was the longest two mile drive of my life, and as each second ticked by, my chest grew tighter, and my hands trembled faster. I didn't think it possible that my level of terror and anxiety could have risen beyond what I had already experienced that morning. But the fear was getting worse. I was at level 9 -- no doubt about it.

Once back at the top, the officer let me out of the car and pointed at the ground.

"Now stay here until the tow arrives."

"OK, I promise. I will," I lied again.

As his car disappeared below the crest, my panic peaked. Instead of running north like I had done the first time, this time I decided to simply run south. It didn't matter what the officer had told me, I needed to get off that bridge -- *immediately.*

The terror and panic that rolled in waves through my body was taking its toll, and exhaustion and paranoia were setting in. I started to see police cars everywhere -- dozens of them -- at least that was what I thought. Perhaps I was hallucinating. But before long, the lights from a second, very real New Jersey State Police car were flashing in front of me, and another officer was walking in my direction.

By now I was sure I looked like I was completely out of my mind. And if he thought that, too, he would have been right. I couldn't have blamed him if he had pulled his revolver, or even shot at me.

But I was fortunate that the officer remained professionally calm, and we walked through the same conversation I had already had with his colleague. And he also insisted that I had to remain with my vehicle.

"And what if I don't?" I asked.

"*I don't give two shits about what you're saying. Lock me up, I don't give a crap,*" I thought.

"You need to either stay with your truck, or you will have to come with me to the station house," he insisted.

"I'm sick, sir. You can take me back to my truck if you want to, but I am not going to stay on top of that bridge!"

There was no way I was going to tell him I was afraid. I was bigger than him and tougher than him, and I was not going to admit weakness, tell him about my panic attacks, my throat closing up or the hospital exits. How could he understand that? I didn't understand that.

An overhead shot of the world's busiest bridge.

Plus, it was somewhat of a strategic move. There was no way I was going to stay with that truck, and I knew that if I ran again, I would be arrested anyway. It seemed like a good idea to just cut to the chase.

I was placed in the back of the squad car and off we went to the Secaucus, New Jersey Police Barracks. I didn't care about my appointment anymore; in fact, I don't think I cared about anything. But I was grateful. I was drenched in sweat and felt sick and I knew if I passed out there, the officers would simply rush me to the nearest hospital. I started to feel safer. I began to calm down.

At the station, I told them I was just a businessman with a fear of heights. I said I simply couldn't stay on top of a bridge. That was it -- heights. Afraid of heights. Yeah, right.

It was the biggest lie of all. I wasn't afraid of heights -- I was afraid of everything!

I know I can't change the past, but I do have one wish.

I wish I could go back and tell the terrified guy on that bridge everything I have learned since then, everything I know now.

But maybe I can try.

2

DOCTORS

It is easy to be brave from a safe distance.

~Aesop

The typical dictionary definition for an anxiety and panic attack sounds something like this:

"...an acute psychobiologic reaction manifested by intense anxiety and panic. Symptoms include heart palpitations, shortness of breath, dizziness, faintness, profuse diaphoresis, pallor of the face and extremities, gastrointestinal discomfort, an intense feeling of eminent doom or death.

Attacks usually occur suddenly, last from a few seconds to an hour or longer, and vary in frequency from several times a day to once a month. Prolonged panic and anxiety can cause agoraphobia which is a condition where the person is afraid to leave his/her so-called safe place..."

But for most of my adult life, I just called it "The Thing."

That unforgettable day on that bridge on the New Jersey Turnpike was the kind of experience I have endured my whole life. The Thing scared the shit out of me. It was terrifying. It was humiliating. It was debilitating. And unfortunately, there would be many more incidents to come.

As far back as I can remember, from my teen years into my twenties, I would experience these panic attacks but didn't know how to describe these feelings to anyone. Maybe it was because I didn't want to look foolish -- I have always valued strength and found it shameful to not be in control of myself. And since I really didn't know what was wrong with me anyway, I learned that blaming my health -- especially my heart -- could be the perfect scapegoat.

I remember sitting in hospitals and in doctors' offices many times while the doctors focused intently around the performance of my heart and my irregular heart palpitations. Heart problems always make doctors a little skittish. Many times the emergency room doctors would keep me there for hours hooked up to all sorts of wires and EKG machines, carefully monitoring my blood pressure and my heart rate, making certain all was fine before they dared let me leave. And I admit I was not being totally honest with them. I couldn't tell them that my heart problems always revolved around this profound fear. I needed to convince them there was more of a physical reason. You see, if I acknowledged the fear, it would reveal a chink in my armor. I could not accept that. There would be no chink.

Through the years, I have had many hospital visits and most of the time they were short, because as soon as I arrived, I'd immediately feel the relief of help being near, and I would begin to calm down. Through all my hospital visits, I never had a doctor tell me I was experiencing anxiety or panic attacks. Never. Not once. Though it's disappointing to know that so many of our best medical professionals didn't immediately recognize the symptoms of a panic attack when they evaluated me, I know that I am partly to blame for that. I admit I never gave them all the right information they needed to pour into their proverbial diagnosis blender. It was too embarrassing. When asked, my answers to their questions were usually the same vague explanations.

> *"No Doc, nothing really happened."*
> *"I really don't know what's wrong with me."*
> *"No, I didn't have 12 cups of coffee."*
> *"Yes, I promise to get my heart checked by my family doctor as soon as I get home."*

When I was younger, I was once prescribed beta blockers to help with the palpitations. Beta blockers are drugs often given to cardiac patients to treat heart palpitations, angina, high blood pressure and other related conditions. I took them for a while but deep down I knew that they weren't treating the problem -- or should I say treating the root of the problem. So I just stopped taking them.

And I once had a nurse ask me if I was seeing a psychologist, accusing me of bringing this all on myself. Was this all self-inflicted? Was I crazy? I was into my late twenties at the time, and was spending lots of time alone as my wife was frequently on the road working as a flight attendant for Eastern Airlines. I remember leaving the office and spending a long evening lost in my own thoughts, not arriving back at home from the hospital until five o'clock that morning feeling deeply depressed. Because how could I, the proud, strong man I was, be doing all this to myself on purpose? Could the nurse be right?

Almost no one wants to admit that they are seeing a psychiatrist, but I did, once, when I was in my thirties. After listening to my stories, he came to the conclusion that I was a victim of my own ego feeding upon itself. I don't know if he realized that I was suffering from anxiety and panic or not, as he never actually used those words. But he did give me a homework assignment. He asked me to read Tom Wolfe's novel, *A Man in Full*. I remember that as I was reading this book I was wondering why, out of all the books in the world, he gave me this book to read. If you aren't familiar with it, the story is essentially about a man with a lot of ego trying to be everything to everyone. He had a good ego and a bad self-destructing ego. I figured I must have an awful lot of this last one.

But did this explain why I can't be even alone with myself? Why I can't go through tunnels or speak in front of people? Why I fear bridges, traffic or can't just be alone with my thoughts? Or worse? So it's all my ego? Is that the cause?

Did this explain why in Manhattan, while staying over after partying late at a friend's house, I would tie my wrists to the armrest of the couch with a bathrobe tie at 4:30 in the morning because at that point, the anxiety was so bad I did not know if I would jump from his high-rise or not? I have never, ever entertained a single suicidal thought in my life, but I wasn't sure if The Thing wouldn't make me jump anyway, or more accurately, push me. I would experience over a hundred different uncontrollable feelings -- all negative -- shooting through my head at the same time. All of these feelings, while clearly psychological, caused many physical problems. And once the physical problems kicked in -- heart palpitations, sweaty palms, hands shaking like a leaf -- then my brain would take over with deep feelings of panic. Many people who have known me for years would say I seemed to be sick all the time, that I always seemed to suffering with a cold or the flu. And I did -- all this stress would cause my immune system to simply crash. It's medically proven. It was a terribly vicious cycle, and it still is. And without the right tools to know how to combat it, it's a horrible way for anyone to go through life.

It is not an out-of-control ego. It is not self-inflicted. It is agoraphobia.

To sufferers of agoraphobia, horrible thoughts come to you no matter where you are -- fear of passing out when driving a car, or on the train in front of people, or in church walking up to communion, or in public places like restaurants, supermarkets, malls -- basically everywhere. It's fear of leaving your safe place.

I used to test myself and see how far I could walk through a store and stand in the back without looking at an exit or for an exit sign. Little did I know that this was the wrong way to go about it. Constantly fighting with yourself is not the way to deal with anxiety and panic. The first step toward fixing this affliction is to just let it happen, feel the fear, accept it, and learn exactly what it is all about. Once you learn the nature of the beast, you will be able to control it in a very intelligent way.

Without any formal medical help, I created my own system of scoring these panic attacks on a 1 to 10 scale. My panic attack on the New Jersey Turnpike ranked a 9, while my panic attack in my friend's apartment a mere 7. I have never experienced a 10, though I have often wondered what it would be like, and if I could survive it.

And because of this, *scared to death, do it anyway* has become my motto.

One out of ten people suffer from this disorder in the United States. If you are one of them, please understand that although it may feel like it, you are not alone.

Now let me tell you how I was able to overcome it.

3

THE INNOCENT

When one has the feeling of dislike for evil, when one feels tranquil, one finds pleasure in listening to good teachings; when one has these feelings and appreciates them, one is free of fear.

~ Buddha

To fully understand someone, it's always good to learn about where they came from and what they were all about -- what makes them tick. For me, to understand where these panic and anxiety attacks originated and how I was able to overcome them, I think it would be helpful to hear a little about my childhood. And that's not because something horrific, traumatizing or extraordinary happened -- it's because for the most part, it didn't.

I was born in Cranford, New Jersey in 1961 and our family lived in Dunellen (a suburb of Plainfield) in the central part of the state. Dunellen was a typical small city -- barely a square mile wide with plenty of parks and easy access to the highway and very near the metropolis of New York City.

My dad was a blue-collar, hard-working guy who fit right in with the makeup of the neighborhood. In fact, I remember him always working two jobs as long as we lived there. My mother also worked a part-time job to help make ends meet, but she was far more interested in raising her kids. Both my parents grew up in Brooklyn in the 1950's, and embraced the traditional, classic American values of that era and were eager to use them to raise their own family.

When I turned five, I was sent to kindergarten at St. Mary's, the local Catholic school, where I would stay enrolled until 1969. During that time, even as a young boy, I could feel the racial tension of the day as I walked through the hallways. I remember feeling the stress and anxiety it brought even though I didn't understand it. Even at this age, I remember being in tune to anxiety and insecurity. I felt anxiety all the time. How could I possibly know that this was so unusual?

I remember one embarrassing incident quite clearly. I was only in second grade, and we had been assigned a very difficult project that involved cutting a picture from one page and pasting it in the right place on another. And of course, I had somehow completely misunderstood the assignment and instead, colored in the area that was supposed to be glued. In Catholic school, they would call out each of us by name and have us come up to the nun at the front of the class to have the work examined and checked off. Although I was a very likable kid, and had many friends in the class, I absolutely hated to stand up in front of all my schoolmates. I could not bear that kind of attention.

When I realized the mistake in my assignment, I panicked. I didn't have any glue, so I scribbled with my yellow crayon as hard and frantically as I could until the waxy build-up was thick and sticky, and then I pressed the picture into the right place, hoping it would stick long enough to have the project approved and let me return to my desk unnoticed. I prayed that this last-minute fix would get me through. Even at just seven years old, I can remember all the classic symptoms and stages of anxiety and panic attacks coming on -- sweating, heart palpitations, shaking -- but back then, to me, this was normal.

As my bad luck would have it, I was the last student in my row to be called. All I needed was for Sister Mary to look at it for five seconds and I'd get my check mark. I could feel my throat closing as I presented my work to the nun. But the waxy yellow crayon just wouldn't hold like glue, and my hastily-attached little picture slipped off and fell helplessly to her desk. The nun scowled, pointed her crooked finger, and ordered me to stand in shame at the front of the class.

I was so terrified that I lost control of myself and shit my pants.

I stood there in absolute terror and shame as the nun checked off the remainder of my classmates' work, then she turned her attention back to me, slashed a ruler across the back of my hand and ordered me to take my seat.

I returned to my seat as instructed, in a swirl of pain and embarrassment, my eyes welled with tears... and I was starting to really stink. As the nun was preparing for the next lesson, she spun her head, crumpled up the bridge of her nose and asked,

Did somebody crap their pants?

And of course, every finger in the room pointed at me.

As I reflect back, I know two things for sure: first, there's no doubt the incident helped enhance my social anxiety and second, though I liked school, it was the first step in a future of really, really hating schoolwork.

I have always been a pleaser. I remember at a very early age wanting to please both my father and mother, and I always looked for reassurance and I enjoyed feeling that I had made them proud. Whether it was fixing a mailbox, shoveling snow, or just cleaning up after a birthday party, I thrived on their approval. There was nothing in this world more important to me.

I was constantly looking for ways to help my dad with anything I could.

But with my classmates, the only I way I could get their approval, or so I thought, was to make them laugh. So as odd as it was for a kid to hate being the center of attention, I would often talk out of turn. At St. Mary's, we had to go to church every day, and if you got caught talking, a 250-pound nun would make a fist and plant it in your back so hard the whole church would vibrate. I was on the receiving end of that punishment more than once.

In the summer of 1969, my father came home one afternoon and announced that he had been offered a new job at a medical plastics company called Becton Dickinson in Canaan, Connecticut. Because of the rising racial tensions and crime in our city at the time, I learned he had been looking to relocate our family for quite a long while.

And what a wonderful culture shock it would be for an eight-year-old boy!

Suddenly, we were living in a wonderful ranch house with three acres of land. For a little city boy like me, moving to Canaan was absolute heaven -- the school was big, yards were big, and there was... freedom! There were even 10,000 acres of land behind my new house called Canaan Mountain, and I would come to explore every square inch of it.

Enjoying a summer day in Canaan, Connecticut.

I believe that our time spent living in Canaan to be the best time of my life. I was able to make many new friends, play outside until after dark every night, and with the help of all the older kids in our new neighborhood, I learned how to make go-carts out of wagons, ride mini-bikes, play baseball, play pond hockey and overall, just have a hell of a great time running around in the woods.

I also learned a lot about myself -- I learned I loved to be alone.

One of my favorite pastimes was to build a fort out in the woods and just sit inside it for hours. Here I was safe, secure and relaxed. Inside my fort everything was great, and all was always well in this world.

But despite my love for our new home, the great friends I was making and the safe haven I was building around me, the anxiety and uneasiness was growing and becoming more of a constant struggle. And Sundays were always the worst.

On Sunday nights, my parents would often go out on errands and to the movies together, and leave me alone with my older sister Laura and younger brother Steven. I remember being relaxed and watching that classic 70's TV line-up of *The Lawrence Welk Show, Wild Kingdom,* and *The Wonderful World of Disney* and suddenly feel my throat start to close. I could feel the panic rise the moment they said they were heading out the door. Even my forts couldn't help me ease the anxiety, because with my parents away, my home base had vanished. In my mind, I would be silently praying for them to stay, and I remember being very upset. They had no way to know the severity of the attacks I was dealing with, and how every time they left, the anxiety deepened. Though I wanted them to stay, I didn't want them to know why. And I'm not sure I could have explained it anyway.

Anxiety and panic feeds on itself in a vicious cycle, and when you are a child, you don't possess any of the tools you need to deal with and handle these situations. It was on these Sunday nights that I first started to believe there was something terribly wrong with me -- all the time. Why did I do this to my parents? I was a pleaser -- I couldn't bear to upset them. I did not understand. The guilt and embarrassment was starting to build.

Towns like Canaan tend to be very safe places. There are no strangers, as everybody knows everybody else. Yet still, I felt constantly uneasy.

I loved being a Boy Scout, but absolutely hated Boy Scout camp. I enjoyed all the activities during the day, but at night, I was terrified that something terrible was going to happen to me. The anxiety I felt was overwhelming yet I did not dare show it. I remember many instances of creating excuses about things I had to go and do whenever I heard there would be a sleepover coming up.

Tommy was one of my best friends, and he and his family lived on a huge 20-acre lot that had a camper on site. I loved hanging around with Tommy, but I hated sleeping over in his camper, and couldn't bear to say anything to him or anyone about it. Again, I wasn't afraid of the walls closing in, or werewolves, or maniacs coming out of the forest to attack us, I was simply afraid of my own thoughts. This was the period of my life when the "*what ifs*" began:

> "*What if my throat closes?*"
> "*What if I can't breathe?*"
> "*What if I pass out?*"
> "*What if...?*"

Embarrassment had taken control of my life.

Looking back on it now, although I have so many great childhood memories, I regret not having more. Now decades later, it's still easier to remember the fear.

4

EMERGENCY!

*D*ispatcher: *Squad 51, informant reports toxic chemicals in the tanker, use caution.*

Dr. Kelly Brackett: *Squad 51, this is Rampart. Can you send us some EKG?*

John Gage: *Ten-four, we're transmitting EKG. We're sending you a strip. Vitals to follow. Pulse is 160, the ictim is in extreme pain, Rampart. V-fib!*

Paramedic Roy DeSoto: *Patient is in V-fib! Rampart, we have lost the victim's pulse, beginning CPR. We're defibrillating victim, Rampart. Rampart, we have defibrillated victim, he has sinus rhythm.*

Joe Early: *Administer two amps Sodium Bicarb. Insert an airway. Start an IV, 51 - Lactate Ringer's.*

Dixie McCall: *Squad 51, continue to monitor patient and transport immediately.*

John Gage: *We're on our way, Rampart.*

> ~ From the opening credits to the TV show *Emergency!*

If you are old enough, you might remember the TV show *Emergency!* from the 70's. It starred Randolph Mantooth and Kevin Tighe as paramedics who would put their lives on the line every week while running around Los Angeles saving dying people and rushing them to the hospital.

Oh my God, I hated that show.

It was a great television show for a kid -- action, suspense, police cars, fire engines. What wasn't to like? But for me, I couldn't watch any TV show about the medical profession. The minute Gage and DeSoto showed up at the scene, and the victim was either passed out, hyperventilating, dizzy, unconscious, feeling chest pain, hallucinating, or experiencing any one of a hundred other symptoms, my anxiety level would shoot through the roof. I would believe: *Hey, that's me! That's what I have! I'm going to pass out, get rushed to the hospital and die just like them!*

To be honest, my dislike of *Emergency!* extended to any and all hospital TV shows, or any other drama that over the course of telling its story found its way into a hospital or doctor's office. I couldn't watch any of those programs without believing the victim on each show was me.

Thank God I didn't have the Internet or WebMD when I was growing up!

Panic and anxiety attacks are a mental problem first and physical problem second. However, I can tell you firsthand that the pain and physical symptoms at times would become so intense that

I truly believed I was dying from some serious disease. When you don't know what you have or what's wrong, your brain has the tendency to search until it finds what it thinks is the most logical answer. It's looking for its "aha" moment.

Every time your eyes begin to burn or your stomach starts to ache, you start to hope there is something physically wrong with you and that you now have the symptoms that will prove it. When you don't know what you have, your anxiety becomes magnified because you believe your body is out of control. You find yourself in a constant search for answers, and anything you can latch onto helps ease your stress. You pray you'll discover the "aha" moment again, because that last "aha" moment, though it provided temporary relief, didn't work out so well.

Ironically, every time you get sick, it comes with an unexpected feeling of relief. *Yes! Thank goodness I'm sick! There really is something wrong with me! I feel like this because I have XYZ Disease!* The Thing had become something with a name that I could now explain, understand, and control.

But sadly, after every illness, something terrible would happen -- I would get better.

I admit this is hard to understand, but I guarantee that people who suffer silently from this affliction know exactly what I'm talking about. They pray to find the real reasons behind their thoughts and their thinking and look for answers around every corner, including every TV show.

At this time in my life, I'm actually happy to report that my condition is not a disease you can treat with a drug or a pill. I once hoped it would be like diabetes where you could simply inject a bit of insulin in your arm to monitor your sugar levels and make you feel better.

But that's not yet the case with severe anxiety. It has been proven that there are many chemicals in the brain, like serotonin, that influence mood and feelings, and every one of us possesses different levels of them naturally. There is also a part of the brain called the amygdala that controls anxiety, aggression, and the fight or flight response, and responds one way in some people, yet entirely differently in others. These are the physical origins for anxiety and panic attacks. Doctors and scientists are still studying them to understand how they fit together and work. If they happen to be broken, there is no pill to fix them.

But this doesn't matter. When it all comes down to it, it is still very possible to beat it, and I don't mean by fighting. I have learned that it sometimes is best to just let the beast be.

An exact replica of the famous rescue vehicle from the 70's TV show Emergency! *I hated that show.*

5

STRENGTH

I want a ballplayer with guts enough not to fight back.
~ Branch Rickey to Jackie Robinson, in the movie "42"

When I was ten years old, I bought a booklet in a penny candy store in Canaan, Connecticut that featured a picture of a man standing with his arms up holding a barbell over his head. This guy looked incredibly powerful and his muscles were gigantic! The booklet offered detailed information on getting strong and promised that if the instructions were followed, I would look just like him.

At ten, I had already recognized that there was something wrong with me. And I remember thinking to myself that all my problems -- the nervousness, the fear, the panic, the anxiety -- were all because I was a scrawny, little, weak kid. I convinced myself that if I followed the advice in this booklet and got stronger, I would be bigger and tougher and all my fears and problems would just melt away. Easy.

The weightlifting booklet that changed my life and started me on a lifetime of working out.

I took the booklet home and read it cover to cover, then I read it again. I immediately began doing push-ups and sit-ups just like it said I should. We didn't own a set of weights, but I was still able to do many of the strength-training exercises (better known today as dynamic workout) in their place. I would work on the muscles in my chest, my arms, my back and my shoulders every single day. When my parents' friends came to visit, I'd work through my routine alone in my room, then prance around the house with my shirt off waiting for someone to comment how big I looked. They always did, but I assume they said it just to appease me. I looked pretty much the same as I always had.

I suppose I was driving my father nuts at this point, so he went out and bought me a beautiful new set of weights so I could do the exercises outlined in the book properly. I dove into the exercises with enthusiasm, and for about two months, I lifted and curled those weights every day. But just like most impatient kids of that age, I became frustrated when I didn't get the results I wanted right away. I lost interest and traded the weights for a banana bike. I think my dad wanted to kill me.

My new school in Canaan was five times the size it had been in New Jersey, and there were a lot of big kids around. I wanted so bad to not only fit-in "size wise" but to be normal, not my usual nervous self. And then my father, who was always trying to do better, received an offer to manage a blow molding company in Providence, RI, and he accepted it. I was leaving Canaan. I felt sick to my stomach. I bawled my eyes out. It was paradise for a kid: mountains, little girl crushes, baseball, fishing and neighborhood friends. It sucked! I remember those feelings to this day. Even my favorite Saturday morning ritual of taking trash to the dump with my dad would end. Little did I know it would be for the best in the future.

Then when we moved to Rhode Island there were even more big kids, and it felt to me that all the other kids were growing and getting bigger while I remained small.

The first friend I made at my new school in Rhode Island was named Bill. He was a neighborhood kid who thought I was pretty cool. It didn't take me long to figure out Bill didn't have many friends and was terrible at sports. I think he was drawn to me because I was the new kid and because I was small and obviously wasn't one of the cool kids. All the cool kids were big, looked tough and played sports. One of those kids was a tough, scary-looking kid named Reggie who wore an army jacket all the time and smelled awful. He was big, and also a star member of the school's wrestling team.

One day in gym class, the teacher announced our activity that day would be wrestling. And of course with my luck, I was randomly matched up against Reggie who not only outweighed me by at least 25 pounds, but he also smelled like pot and cigarettes. I was scared shitless. As expected, he pinned me to the mat in less than two seconds. I really had no idea how to fight him off, and as I was going down, I blindly thrust my palms up into his face and struck him square in the nose. It was an accident, but that didn't stop a sudden burst of blood from shooting across the mat. Reggie was humiliated, furious, and fully prepared to destroy me. The gym teacher dove in quickly and broke us up. Thank God. If there had been a real fight, I probably would have been killed.

Back in Canaan, my younger brother and I had many neighborhood friends with whom we used to play baseball almost every day in the summertime. Skirmishes within our groups of friends were normal -- boys will be boys as they say. Whenever my brother would get into a squabble with any one of my friends, I would always come to his aid ready to fight. But I would pray to myself it wouldn't come to real fisticuffs. I might have acted and looked tough, but inside, I was terrified.

One of my best friends at that time was named Nate, and he was the toughest kid in our group. His parents had divorced and I remember he carried around a ton of anger. The second toughest kid in town was Jimmy, and he was twice the size of Nate. I remember Jimmy starting something with me one time, and I remember Nate jumping to my defense and smashing Jimmy square in the face. I'll never forget how scared I was or forget the humiliated look displayed across Jimmy's face as he ran home. A few days later, my brother mouthed off at Nate during a pick-up basketball game. It was just a war of words until for some reason, my brother decided it would be a great idea to spit at him. Nate totally lost it -- and charged him. My brother hopped on his bike and rode away, leaving me behind, per the code of the neighborhood, to defend his honor. I chased Nate down as I was expected to, but I did not hit him. I just begged and pleaded with him to please just leave my little brother alone. Nate did eventually cool off and back down but I will never forget that sensation of crippling fear that knotted itself in the pit of my stomach. If Nate had turned around to me and said, "*OK, let's go,*" I don't know what I would have done. I am grateful he didn't.

Now here I was years later, a freshman in high school nose to nose with Reggie, face bloodied, looking me square in the eye uttering that same phrase: "*OK. Let's go -- after class.*" It was like having to fight Nate all over again. A terror like that is all too easy to recall, and even though now I was older, I was just as scared and just as nervous. And with only two or three friends in the whole school to protect me against Reggie's army of potheads, I was doomed. My mother would pick me up after school on occasion, and Reggie would see me as he walked past and would flip me off. My mother was alarmed, and asked what was going on, and of course I would shrug it off and say he was just some odd, new friend. Reggie had the reputation for starting many fights, and finishing them very quickly. My goal was to avoid Reggie everywhere, all the time, at all costs.

I was a scared, panic-stricken kid with zero confidence. I was now living in day-to-day survival mode. To get out of fighting Reggie, I had to blend in with the rest of the kids and disappear -- like a chameleon. I learned that when I hung around with the nerds, I could look and act like a nerd. When I hung around with the potheads, I could look and act like a pothead. When I hung around with the jocks, I could look and act like a jock. To my surprise, this chameleon act helped me become more popular with everybody -- including a lot of girls. It's funny how fear and anxiety drove me to adapt and become a relationship-driven person. It would be a skill I would carry into business and sales and use for decades to come.

And by the way, I never did need to fight Reggie; in fact, we became friends.

I made another new friend then, too. He loved to work out, and was a motorhead with a great car, so a bunch of us would pile in and go to a nearby gym to train. Although I had given away my weights long ago, that desire to increase my physical strength had never left me. I never did throw away that little booklet I bought at the candy store, and in fact, still have it tucked away safely to this day. By the time I reached my junior year in high school, I had gained 20 to 25 pounds of muscle. I was also getting stronger and could bench press 315 pounds. I finally felt like I was becoming one of the guys. My confidence was slowly building along with my popularity.

I dated many different girls, bought my own car, and made the football team. During my senior year in high school, I was lifting more weights than ever before. It was also an era when steroids were starting to become popular, but I never used them. I would guess that if I wasn't afflicted with a panic and anxiety disorder, I may have used them right along with everybody else. But the thought of putting something inside my body that I could not control brought on a whole other level of anxiety I couldn't begin to deal with. I was lucky. Many of the kids I worked out with back then tried and stayed on steroids. And I know for a fact it killed some of them.

I loved to work out. The gym became my second home. The stronger I got, the more confidence I felt, and the less anxiety I felt. I perceived that being a strong man would be a hedge against the panic. But how strong is strong? There were times when I felt like that strength needed to be tested.

I got hurt during a football practice, dislocated my elbow and shoulder, and was forced to stand on the sidelines one Saturday to watch our team play. When halftime ended, I walked with the team back to the field from the locker room when someone from the opposition's grandstands cat-called down at me.

"Hey punk! You suck!"

Even though I had one arm in a sling, I glared back at him with all the self-assurance in the world. I responded confidently.

"Fuck you!"

The kid flew down out of the grandstands toward me and I heard those magic words once again.

"Oh yeah? You want to go?"

I was strong. I was cool. I was pumped and by this time I had been in and even won a few fights. And oh hell yes, I did. I did want to go.

The two of us walked into the end zone and fists flew. The adrenaline was pumping through my veins with such force that my badly-injured arm didn't hurt a bit. Before too long, the teams had completely emerged from the locker rooms and surrounded us, the referees had returned, and the police who had been watching the game in the crowd were restoring order. It was the first time in my life I was upset someone had stopped me from fighting.

And then, two years later, I was working out alone in the gym when a guy I had seen in there before asked me to "spot" for him (to keep an eye on his weights while he lifted). Son of a bitch if it wasn't that guy I fought that day in the end zone!

The guy's name was Danny, and to this day, I am proud to say we are the best of friends -- we're as close as brothers. As strong as I am now and as successful as I would be in subsequent fights, I am glad we didn't finish that one that day. Danny is probably the toughest son of a bitch I have ever known. We became weightlifting partners and I can say without a doubt that Danny has made me both mentally and physically tougher than I could ever have been training by myself; he brought out the lion in me. We pushed each other in the gym harder than anyone on this planet ever could, and sometimes, it would even end with the two of us in a fistfight. By now I weighed over 200 pounds, could bench press close to 400 pounds, could squat 500 pounds and deadlift 600 -- all completely natural. We were maniacs in the gym. It was my sanctuary.

Danny also suffered from an anxiety problem but he had a better reason than me -- he was a guard in the worst part of the local prison. He was 5'9" and carried 220 pounds of solid muscle everywhere he went. He was the guy everyone would call when things got out of hand with an inmate. He confided in me that he felt unbearable anxiety every time he knew there would be a physical confrontation at work. But the fighting and physical interaction helped him deal with and release that anxiety. It was a product of the natural human fight or flight response. And since it was his career, job, and the safety of his fellow guards on the line, flight wasn't ever an option. Once the adrenaline starts to flow, it flows. That's what happens in a fight. Danny says he has never lost a fight in his life. And I believe him.

Although it's OK to push yourself through anxiety and panic attacks in the gym, you can't get away with that in real life.

When on business trips later, I would call Danny from my hotel room in the middle of a panic attack. I would be a total mess. I remember *The Tonight Show with Johnny Carson* would be going off the air and I knew I would have to shut off the lights at some point. I'd call Danny at home and he would talk me through the moment in a very soft-spoken but tough way. He was sort of like that trainer in the corner every boxer hopes for: *You can do this shit. Don't be a fucking pussy. Deal with it. Nothing's going to happen to you. Fight, Brian. Fight! Fight!*

The words and phrases he used were the same words I would roll over and over in my own mind for years to come during all sorts of attacks. But looking back on it now, I've learned it's exactly what you must *not* do. I didn't realize then that you can't fight anxiety, because it feeds on the same flash of adrenaline you need to fight it. It's not like facing the Reggies, or the Nates or the Dannys of the world -- they are real, physical entities standing in front of you. The scary thoughts I needed to fight were evolving deep inside my own mind and would grow when I closed my eyes. I would rather lose a dozen physical fights with anyone than be forced to fight against the incredible scary and terrifying sensations the human body is capable of producing.

Accept the anxiety. Develop the strength not to fight back. It is the first step in the healing thought process.

6

THE SKI TRIP FROM HELL

Consult not your fears but your hopes and your dreams. Think not about your frustrations, but about your unfulfilled potential. Concern yourself not with what you tried and failed in, but what it is still possible for you to do.

~Pope John XXIII

Anxiety has a wretched, heartbreaking habit of ruining your favorite activities by turning them into something frightening. I watched helplessly as all the things I learned to love and enjoy throughout my childhood slowly began to manifest themselves differently as I grew older. Finding reality became part of every activity I chose to undertake. Was I going to enjoy doing it as I always had, or would the anxiety drive me to hate this, too?

Entering my teenage years, my panic and phobias had reached an all-time high leaving me in a state of constant ready-alert. There are many unfortunate incidents and examples I could talk about that would illustrate my point here, but there was one weekend that will always stay at the forefront of my mind that covers it all quite well. I think of it as the ski trip from hell.

I was only sixteen, and one day my friend Joe called out of the blue and asked, "Hey Brian, what do you say we get the guys together and go up to New Hampshire for the weekend, rent a place and do some skiing?"

"Oh, yea! I am in!" I answered. I loved to ski. But I couldn't possibly let Joe know that the thought also absolutely terrified me. His offer was a torment.

Oh shit! Now I have to drive all the way to New Hampshire, stay in some fucking cabin in the middle of nowhere with no help available for miles. Then they'll see their buddy Brian -- the cool, tough, weightlifter -- fall apart and humiliate himself. Oh yeah, this is going to be a blast.

We picked the worst possible time to leave -- five o'clock on a Friday afternoon -- and fought traffic all the way through Massachusetts into New Hampshire. All the great 80's rock bands like Boston and Kansas played on the radio as we travelled, and we sang along like we were on stage somewhere. The music, and the case of beer we bought for the ride, helped keep my pals cool and mellow; and that helped me cope quite a lot with the building stress. And yes, I was driving. I couldn't possibly let anyone else be in control.

The Kancamagus Highway snakes its way for almost 60 miles around, over, and through New Hampshire's White Mountain National Forest. It's a tricky drive during the day in the summertime, never mind at night in the winter. The farther along the highway I drove, the higher my anxiety level rose... 5... 6... 7. I did a great job of keeping a fake smile pasted across my face even though my heart was racing at 100 miles per hour. What the hell happens if I pass out and we crash into those trees, I thought, or go over these guardrails and plunge into an icy ravine?

We stopped for food at around ten o'clock. I felt like I had been driving for days, and hadn't seen a set of oncoming headlights in over an hour. I prayed that we had to be close. I didn't think I could drive much more.

"How much longer, Joe? We almost there?"

"Yea, almost. Only about another hour and a half."

An hour and a half? Fuck me. We are all totally screwed.

But somehow, I bore down and we eventually made it. There was a second car that was following us that night that became hopelessly lost along the trip (of course there were no GPS units or cell phones back then), and arrived hours later after stopping several times to ask for directions. What Joe didn't know was that I didn't need directions. A good, card-carrying agoraphobic always does his research and memorizes exactly where he is going before he leaves his house. As we pulled into the parking lot, I looked ahead and couldn't believe my luck -- our rental was right next door to a hospital. Yes! Instantly, I felt a rush of relief and my anxiety level dropped like a stone. It even put me in a good mood, and after we tossed our bags into our rooms, we all came together in the kitchen for another round of beer, shots and air guitar. We partied and acted like complete fools until about 1:30 when everyone finally burned out and started to crash.

I disappeared into my room alone. Some might think that with panic and anxiety problems, having friends around at night would help. But for me, it was just the opposite. These guys were my best friends who I hung out with almost every Friday night. If I was forced to get up in the middle of the night and act like a complete fool, I had to make sure none of them would be around to witness my embarrassment.

I only slept about three and a half hours when as expected, a level 9 panic attack spiked out of nowhere. I learned later on that alcohol masks anxiety. But as you sober up it bounces back like a rubber band to excruciating levels. It was the middle of winter and I was bathed in sweat. I couldn't stop thinking about being alone out there in the middle of the wilderness. I looked out the window and couldn't see a single light. I monitored and counted every breath -- in and out, in and out -- and sincerely feared I would slip into some kind of insanity. The only thought that seemed to help was knowing that the hospital was just a half mile down the road. But then I started thinking.... what if I run out the door toward that hospital and don't make it? How would they know that I was lost out there somewhere in the middle of the woods? My friends would probably assume I had hooked up with a girl somewhere; they'd never even try to look for me!

A gentle brightness on the horizon told me daybreak was approaching, and I quietly slipped out the back door before anyone else was awake. I hopped in the car and drove the half mile down to the hospital, which turned out to be more of a medical clinic of some sort. I didn't want to go in, but just needed to have a look around. I needed to make sure it was really there. The building looked open, but I talked myself out of checking the hours that were posted on the front window. I thought it better to assume and pretend they were open even if they weren't as I wasn't sure I could handle the bad news. Plus, there was a 24-hour food mart next door so I had another place to go if I was in trouble. Just in case. Good enough.

After breakfast we headed over to Wildcat Mountain for our first day of skiing. I loved to ski, and in fact still love to ski, but what I hate is everything else that has to do with skiing. I hate the crowds. I hate the lines. I hate the lifts. I hate the gondolas. I hate the possibility of the gondolas getting stuck. What if! What if!

I also hated the thought of getting lost in the woods and freaking out when I realize I don't know where I am, even though we always skied down the mountain together at least two at a time. It's not a normal type of "lost" sensation that most people might feel, but a sensation of complete and utter panic and what I might do if

I reached level 9 with skis on my feet. Would I just ski straight off the damned mountain?

When we first arrived I was physically shaking from the adrenaline that was coursing through my body, and my friends gave me a hard time, assuming I was having a bad reaction to the cold. "Oh, come on Brian. Look at you! It's not that cold!" I was shaking so bad that when I sat on the chairlift, globs of snow shook loose off the bottom of my skis. I remember looking back behind us every time the chairlift would slow down usually to let a small kid get on. I was so pissed at them all. And God forbid if one of those little kids would fall getting on the chairlift -- what would happen then? What would I do? I had to get off this thing. I was breathing so rapidly that the condensation coming out of my mouth made me look like a smoke stack compared to everyone else.

I snapped this photo while on the chairlift at Wildcat Mountain.

"Is everything OK, man?"

"Yea, of course," I answered. "I feel like shit, though. I think I just partied a little too much last night, that's all." I was lying, smiling, humming to myself and experiencing a panic attack 60 feet in the air. And the lies and pretending always made it much worse.

By the time I got off the chairlift, I was exhausted and hadn't even completed my first run. And just as I felt my anxiety start to ease back from a 9 down to a 7, I realized we were only halfway up the mountain; this was just the midpoint. And of course, all my friends wanted to go all the way to the very top. Sure they did. After all, there was a bar up there.

"So, what do you say, Bri?"

I thought to myself... look, a hill is a hill. If we are here to ski, then let's ski. We don't need to go any higher. And of course, that's exactly what I didn't tell them.

"Yes, that sounds great! Let's get to the top of the mountain!" I shouted.

The second part of the ride up the chairlift was just as excruciating as the first part, and became instantly worse when one of my asshole buddies decided it would be a good idea to swing the chair back and forth. I laughed and pretended it was fun, but deep down, all I could think about was where I would jump off. Every fifteen feet or so I would rationalize that if I jumped here, I could survive and probably only break my legs. I debated if that would be preferable to enduring the panic of swaying in the chair. But I knew that if we stopped and the lift got stuck, there was no way I could sit there for an hour and wait for help to arrive. There was no question I would choose to jump under those circumstances.

It was now only 10:30 in the morning when we arrived at the bar at the top of the mountain, and my God, I needed a drink. After all the Jack Daniels, rum and beer we consumed the night before, our stomachs ached and none of us really wanted to drink anything else, but when you're seventeen and cool, you don't let old-fashioned common sense get in the way. But I drank to help my anxiety subside, not to have fun. So for every one beer my buddies had, I downed three.

Oh yea! Look at Beneduce go!

Our first trip down that day was on one of the most challenging hills on the mountain, a double black diamond trail from top to bottom. It starts with a 12-foot drop and zoom -- you're on your way!

But while I was skiing, I was free. I am a good skier and have no fear or apprehension when gliding down almost any hill at any speed. It's funny, because whether riding dirt bikes or skiing challenging trails, all the fear and anxiety happens either before the fact or after the fact. The "what ifs," "yeah buts," and "oh nos" are products of the subconscious mind. The adrenaline goes right to the roots of your anxiety tree and makes you believe you had no business ever leaving your house, never mind skiing.

The analogy as it relates to adrenaline is the same in the gym. When I was growing up, if you could bench press 315 pounds, then you were the man. There were only two kids in my school who could do it, and they were huge. I weighed a measly 165 pounds. I knew I could bench 300, but whenever I sucked it up and went for 315, the adrenaline rush would be exhilarating. It wasn't the same feeling as the adrenaline rush of a panic attack. It was different. I felt alive. I felt normal.

Normal! That's it! As I raced down that hill, I kept asking myself why I couldn't feel this way all the time? I felt alive. I didn't worry about crashing into trees or wiping out. I honestly felt free for the first time and I was having fun. We did ten or eleven runs that morning before we stopped for something to eat and to brag about what great athletes we all were, *yadda, yadda, yadda.*

But no matter how much fun I was having, the fear and anxiety would always be there lurking in the back of my mind, waiting for its next opportunity to jump out and ruin my day. Just as I was starting to get comfortable with my surroundings and cope with these horrifying lifts, and even have a little fun, some dumb asshole just had to say it.

"Hey... let's go try the gondola!"

Son of a bitch! It's the same damned mountain! That chairlift was just fine!

I thought of a lot of things I wanted to say right then, but of course, I stayed quiet and followed along with the others and got in the 30-yard long line for the gondola trip to the top of the mountain. As we all waited, I tried my best to talk them out of it to no avail, and I quickly resigned myself to the fact that yes, I would have to go through with it.

OK, fine then! Let's all get inside this giant egg-shaped elevator and fly 60 feet off the ground in sub-zero weather. And you'd all better hope we don't stop, because if we do, I plan to throw every damned one of these people off that thing. But hey, yeah, it could be fun.

My anxiety level had never been higher. I counted the giant eggs as they approached the platform -- only twelve to go before I need to get on. The alcohol had started to wear off and I could feel myself starting to go nuts. I thought about how I might be able to fake an injury, or complain that I was about to be sick -- I could tell them it was something I ate, I surmised. Looking back, I should have known I would become some sort of salesman. When I think about all the relationships I've had in my life including my wife, best friends, the bouncers, the bands, the girls I dated -- everybody -- not one of them ever knew the levels of anxiety I was experiencing. I had developed into a terrific actor.

But now I was looking at my friends who were smiling, relaxed and having a good time, and I wanted to smash them each in the face. I was furious. Why can't I be normal like them? Why can't I just enjoy a day of skiing? I wished I could just snap my fingers and transport myself to the top of a mountain. I would dream about dropping out of a helicopter to ski mountains that no one had ever skied before. But then there was the problem of finding a helicopter... and of course the anxiety about getting inside one.

There were now only two groups remaining in front of us ready to board their gondolas. The attendants split up our group so they could fill each of the giant eggs to their maximum capacity. Noticing this, I dropped back a little. If we were going to be split up, I'd much rather be stuck with a group of people I don't know; it's less likely these strangers would ever notice something was wrong with me.

The strategy worked perfectly except for one thing. They packed these things like you'd stuff a bunch of jellybeans into a bag. My timing was so good that when the doors opened, I was the first person to enter my giant egg with a crowd of anonymous skiers pushing me from behind.

"Hey you, get to the back of the car. We have a lot more people to fit in there."

I was a mess. I retreated to the back of the car and tried to cheat to take up as much space as I could get away with. I fought the urge to bolt back through the door and out to safety, but as I debated the idea in my mind, the door slammed closed. I immediately tried to start a conversation with the man squeezed in next to me, but all he did was smile and nod -- then I noticed he had an ear piece and cassette player. I was pissed. I turned around and opened the small window to revive myself with some fresh air, but someone asked if I would please close it -- little Timmy was chilly. I wanted to kill them all. *Son of a bitch.*

The ride was quick and lasted only about three and a half minutes. But I started to visualize what I would do if it suddenly stopped. We were moving along at a very good rate, but I was still having an anxiety attack. I could feel the muscles in my stomach knot up and my heart pound. You could see everyone's breath in the cold air, including mine that looked like a fog machine, but suddenly I realized.... everything was fine! Remember, the "what ifs" tend to come before the activity. It's not the activity itself that causes the anxiety, it's the thought process about the activity that's the root of the problem. Once I was confident that the gondola would not stop mid-route, and I accepted that it only took a few minutes to reach the mountain top, I knew I would be OK. I knew I could do anything for three and a half minutes.

It was a very long day.

Later that night, we were walking through the neighborhood and drinking heavily, heading toward some nameless bar. We could hear music playing and decided to meet up inside. I stuck my beer can in a snowbank and went in the side door

Despite the panic attacks I endured getting to the top of the mountain, I love to ski.

We were all drunk, stupid and happy, but I was more so than anyone else because I could see this trip was soon coming to an end. All we had to do now was make it home. I staggered toward the men's room to take a leak, except I was so smashed, I lost track of where I was and peed on the stage. The place was mobbed, everyone was rocking, and here I was peeing on the bass guitar player. Needless to say, he wasn't happy about it, words were exchanged, and we got into a hell of a fight. It was ugly.

Our visit to the bar lasted no more than twelve minutes and we found ourselves back outside, licking our wounds. And since it was now almost two in the morning, we figured it was about time we walked back to our cottage anyway. (Funny that I couldn't find the bathroom, but knew right where I left my beer in the snowbank.) As we passed the medical center along the way, I noticed they were closed. Next door, the 24-hour food mart was closed, too. I said nothing.

I went back to my room and sat on my bed. I didn't sleep a wink that night. My eyes welled with tears and I rocked back and forth wondering why I couldn't be normal like everyone else. I wanted to feel like that guy who was skiing down the hill earlier that morning. I wanted to feel the exhilaration I did when riding a minibike or like a baseball player when someone hits a ball right at you. You don't become mired in negative thoughts. You just enjoy. You just do. You just live.

I made sure everyone was in agreement that we had to leave early Sunday morning, making up some excuse that I had to get back. I couldn't get stuck driving in the dark again; I just didn't have the energy for it. And I knew what would happen if I had to drive back late -- my reputation would be ruined.

"Hey guys, guess what! Brian shit his pants. It was hilarious... he was just driving back from the ski trip and he just shit his pants!"

"It's irritable bowel syndrome. I have agoraphobia. I didn't even want to leave my house. And by the way, asshole, while you were having a great time all weekend, I was in hell..."

Five hours from home. Please, God, let me get out of New Hampshire and out of these woods and back to reality. Then again, what is reality anyway?

7

THE GYM

Strength does not come from winning. Your struggles develop your strength. When you go through hardships and decide not to surrender, that is strength.

~ Arnold Schwarzenegger

Even when immersed in something you love, anxiety and panic never really leave you. It lurks in the shadows, waiting to show its ugly head to steal all your joy. Powerlifting competitions brought me some of the greatest happiness and because of my agoraphobia, the greatest frustrations I've experienced in my life.

Powerlifting for me is something incredible. It is special. It grew to become a passion and sustaining force in my life.

Powerlifting places *you* against the weight. You can challenge yourself to lift heavier and heavier weights, and, over time you will become stronger and stronger. Unlike bodybuilding where you work out and build muscle only to be judged by other people, the strategy behind powerlifting is more objective: lift heavy, eat more, get bigger, and repeat. It isn't exactly rocket science.

But as a sport, it does offer a compelling simplicity. Milo of Croton was a 6th century Greek wrestling legend known for his amazing strength. He is said to have gained that strength in childhood by carrying a calf across his shoulders every day until the calf grew to maturity. To me, powerlifting embodies that same elegance. Lift 500 pounds today, get stronger, then lift 501 tomorrow. Lift one more pound than the other guy in competition, and you win.

Flex Magazine profiled my Champion Sports Gym in their July 1989 issue.

In 1989, I opened Champion Sports Gym, the largest gym of its kind in Rhode Island to pursue this passion. I loved lifting weights and working out, so going into this business made perfect sense for me and my skills. I quickly became involved with the AAU (Amateur Athletic

Union), the NPC (National Physique Committee), and secured other affiliations while sponsoring a number of regional powerlifting competitions. My gym received a fair amount of positive press, too, once even getting a nice feature write-up in a national publication.

But sadly, I was forced to sell the gym in 1991 to raise money for our plastics company when it started to fail. A few of the machines and remnants of my old gym still exist today in a garage area underneath my current office, taking up space along with other old-school machines I've acquired over the years from well-known gyms around the country.

Even at 54 years old, I still challenge myself in that gym every day -- and some might say to a fault. Because of the injuries I sustained over the years pushing myself too far, the selection of these older machines lets me more easily create my own limits and tailor my own personal workout. This way, I can still "stay heavy."

Back in the day, there were two kinds of powerlifting meets: "natural" and "open." The natural meets meant that you had to pass a drug test in order to be allowed to compete, and as you can imagine, many competitors chose to skip them. The open meets were more popular and indicated that drug testing would not be performed. Since I did not use steroids, or any kind of drugs for that matter, I was welcome to compete in both types of competitions as I saw fit. I was proud to have won several first- and second-place trophies in the natural meets, but one of my favorite trophies was for a fifth-place finish in an open -- I was up against and defeated many of the so-called "juice heads." It was very satisfying.

Some of these meets were held in huge gyms and were controlled chaos with dozens of athletes, spectators and constant activity -- not the ideal atmosphere for someone suffering from anxiety. As a competitor, you essentially stay warm and ready through a very long day. The three lifts a competitor would be expected to perform would be the squat, the bench-press, and the deadlift. Between each exercise you might have to wait two hours. Not good for a person with anxiety. I would stand in the shadows and wait for my name to be announced over the loudspeaker. That announcement was, in essence, a 15-minute warning meaning I was "in the hole" and I needed to warm up and get ready to lift. The second time my name was called, I was "on deck" and expected to lift next. And the third time I was called, I would be expected to walk out and perform.

Honestly, the natural competitions tended to be boring because there just weren't that many competitors. I have never judged my friends who used steroids back then, nor do I fault them for it. They knew it was bad, but the information and available education about performance enhancing drugs wasn't as thorough as it is today. The danger was there but easier to ignore. I'm just glad I didn't go down that path.

I won't easily forget my first open competition.

"Holy shit!" I shouted as my buddy and I strolled into the gym and my anxiety started to stir. "You didn't tell me there would be this many people at this thing. And what the hell is that stage for?"

"The stage? That's where we lift!"

Instant anxiety level five!

It literally took my breath away. I looked at the set-up of weights and the crowd and nearly passed out. It took no time for the "what ifs" to assemble themselves and start marching through my mind. All around me, dozens of huge, muscular, macho, testosterone-filled guys were warming up. I was here as the owner of Champion Sports Gym that had over 2,000 members, had sponsored a world-wide tournament, was gaining notoriety in the business. I was representing my entire group. Was I supposed to tell these guys I couldn't do this, that I was too chicken to walk up on that stage?

Suddenly I heard my name called over the loudspeaker. Damn, I was in the hole and I wasn't mentally prepared for it. I had just fifteen minutes before I would suffer a full-fledged panic attack right here at my first open meet. My mind swirled and my heart pounded. I felt myself losing control.

Then my name was called again. I was on deck. As I wrapped my legs to prepare for my lift, the lifter on stage was grunting and pounding his head against the bar trying to psych himself up. And here I was just trying to keep my legs from shaking. The weight on the bar was pretty low for a first round, but I wasn't worried about that. I was worried about not losing control of my bowels and not passing out in front of these macho guys or the crowd. I wondered if anyone could tell what a mess I was.

Powerlifting is a lot about controlling your breath and using it to your advantage; it was your friend, and here I was losing mine. My throat was closing. I couldn't lift if I couldn't breathe. My breath was rapidly becoming my enemy.

I approached the bar and realized in my haste I had wrapped my knees so tight my feet didn't have any blood circulation. And I was getting lightheaded. I could hear my friends cheering me on, talking in the crowd. Then I heard one of them whisper, "I hope he fucking misses it." Little did I know jealousy and envy never go away.

That bastard. Some friend. But all the voices in the crowd were silenced by the louder voices in my head, the loudest of which was insisting that I fake an injury and head home.

If you do this, Brian, you're going to go down and you're going to embarrass yourself. You won't come up. You'll be lying there right in front of everyone. They'll call the rescue squad and everyone will know there's something wrong with you. You have anxiety and panic, you idiot. What the hell are you trying to prove?

I knew I had lifted this opening weight a hundred times alone, so why can't I do this here in the competition? I got angry. I tried to feed off my panic. I fought off the negatives. I stared over the top of the crowd with 515 pounds on my back, squatted, and lifted. The lift was a success. I looked down into the crowd at my asshole friend who wanted me to fail. I'll let you guess what I said.

I never let him back in my gym. And he won't get a free copy of this book, either.

One lift was good, but I was not done. The competition would be decided after three lifts.

You'd think that after defeating my demons, the second lift would be easier. Not a chance. The anxiety remained, and actually intensified. On my second lift, I used every possible motivator I could think of -- that asshole wanting me to lose, Danny coaxing me on, *Rocky* playing in my head -- but the negative thoughts took over and I could think of nothing but humiliation. But somehow, with 595 pounds on my back, I went down and came up. Another successful lift. That was two.

My third lift was scheduled to be 645 pounds but would not come for another thirty minutes. It was way too much time to think. I faked an injury. I just couldn't do it. I was too emotionally and physically drawn to go through it again. A few days later in the gym, I would lift 660. I could have and should have done it. If I had lifted what I lifted alone in my gym, I would have finished third in my weight class. It would have been an impressive accomplishment. But I wasn't just competing against the strongest men in the area, I had to also compete against my own thoughts. Beating the other powerlifters was hard. In my competition, it was me against me and my anxiety-filled mind, and that was a lot harder.

Agoraphobia steals pleasure. All the things I enjoy in life -- powerlifting, skiing, fishing, boating, camping -- all come packaged with their own phobias and "what ifs" and become entangled and choked by the vines in what I call my "anxiety tree." When you're fishing on a lake and nobody's around, you start thinking... and worrying. When you're on a boat with friends and you see the shore getting farther away, you start thinking... and worrying. And the more you focus and think about the worry, the more activities you avoid, and the more excuses you start to make about why it won't work out, or why you can't go through with it. It's the early stages of agoraphobia -- becoming simply afraid of everything.

By limiting yourself and avoiding the activities you love, you are basically telling yourself that you need to spend the rest of your life in your safe place; you are never allowed to leave and go anywhere else. One key to controlling severe anxiety is to not go to your safe place, but instead, to bring your safe place with you. No matter where I find myself today, or where I am when I feel anxiety start to rise, I know I can reach into my healing thought process toolbox and get myself through the moment. I still suffer from anxiety and panic, and assume I always will, but my anxiety tree is now trimmed and looks like a scrawny weed compared to the mighty tree it once was.

Deep down, there's a contradiction in me that I may never resolve. I'm ashamed of many of the things I loved but didn't do, but I also take great pride in the many things I was able to accomplish in spite of it.

8

GUILT

Guilt is a cancer. Guilt will confine you, torture you, destroy you...
It's a black wall. It's a thief.

~ Dave Grohl

uilt.
Wow, talk about a strong emotion!
Unworthy. Unsure. Not good enough. Worry. Shame.
As a young boy, all I ever wanted to do was make my parents proud; it was what I lived for. But I never did believe I was ever good enough or worthy of receiving that pride. But I must make it very, very clear that this severe guilt trip was not the result of something they said to me, how I was treated, or some unfair expectation that they had created. Quite the contrary, they are great

parents. The source of this profound guilt was created entirely inside my own mind.

Deep feelings of guilt are a significant part of understanding agoraphobia. Guilt is inescapably connected and serves as a catalyst that deepens and enhances fear and anxiety. And because of this, I exist inside a world where I am able to feel guilty about almost every little thing.

No matter how much money I make or what I achieve in life, to this day, I still can't shake all that guilt. I can become envious, jealous and downright angry when I see or hear happy people enjoying themselves. I have wealth, a wonderful wife and two great kids and often can't feel happy about it. It's hard for me to live in the "now" and enjoy myself. Why should I feel guilty? I might be out for a drive in my new sports car or out on my boat on Narragansett Bay, and I will innately take inventory of my family.

What is my son doing? Does he need help? Where is my daughter? Is she OK? If my wife is home worrying about them, then why am I here? What right do I have enjoying myself when they need my help? Maybe I should be making more money right now instead of trying to relax? Shame on me!

Even with the success I have had pruning back my personal anxiety tree, the guilt branches are the longest, thickest and most thorny. They are branches that started growing when I was too young to understand them, and too young to do anything about them.

When I was young, I once remember sitting in the back of our car on vacation with the whole family in Upstate New York. It was late -- sometime after 11 o'clock -- and my mother, sister and brother were all sound asleep as my dad drove up and down the street looking for a decent motel. He would slow the car, squint at the neon *no vacancy* sign, groan, then quickly drive on. He repeated this little routine over and over, and it seemed like there wasn't a single motel in the town where we would be able to check-in that night. I sat in the middle of the back seat with my feet on the wheel well hump and my knees planted under my chin feeding on his mounting frustration, my anxiety rising little by little, moment by moment, until I was a complete mess. I didn't show it, but I was completely in tune to my father's anxiety, and I could sense his frustrations growing in my own mind and body like a cancer. I stared through the windshield and kept my eyes as wide-open as I could, feeling I had a personal responsibility to help our family find a safe place to stay, and I was failing miserably. It hurt and drove me crazy to watch my father worry about anything. I had to help him. I had to try harder. I had no choice.

As I mentioned, my father worked many different jobs when I was little, and if he happened to lose one, I would immediately feel guilty that I hadn't been doing more around the house. I believed I was a burden. How could they be proud of me if I was contributing to my dad's problems? I would feel guilty if my mom served steak for dinner because I knew the household budget was tight; I almost couldn't bear to eat it. When our family went to a restaurant, I would scour the menu and make sure I ordered the cheapest dinner. I hated asking my mom for money for anything even if it was for something important like a school trip. And I knew that if she knew any of this, it would hurt her, too. But I could not be any more of a burden than I thought I already was under any circumstances. I just couldn't do it -- that's just the way it was. It was innate.

As I mentioned, when we moved from Connecticut to Rhode Island, I was crushed. I cried. I loved my friends and old neighborhood and didn't want to move away. It was a very emotional time for every one of us as you can imagine it would be for any family. I was impressed that my sister had the guts to insist she be allowed to go back to Canaan and graduate from her old high school, Housatonic Valley Regional High, with all her friends. I wanted desperately to ask, too, but I couldn't bear the guilt that would have resulted from just posing the question. After all, my father had moved us to this new town to make our lives better. I could not bear to put that added pressure on him.

I worked odd jobs throughout my childhood. I remember selling a newspaper called *Grit* where I would make three or four dollars a week. It wasn't much at all, but in my mind, I was contributing something. At a mere six years old, I would fetch the mail for our elderly neighbor Mrs. Hough and she would give me a quarter. My parents had a Superman bank in their bedroom that was about two feet tall, and I watched my dad put his spare change in it every night. When he wasn't around, I would sneak into his bedroom and slip a few of my own quarters through the slot in the top of Superman's head. I don't know if he ever knew.

When I was a little older, I tried to continue to work as much as I could. I worked at the local swim club and I took a part-time job at the local wiener joint. I really liked to work and make money, but more important than that, it helped ease my guilt and made me feel like I was contributing. In my mind, I was pitching in, even though my mom and dad would never consider actually using my money.

In high school, I worked harder, was paid a little more, and was able to start to save. I worked every day after school that I didn't have sports and I worked almost every weekend. By then my parents were providing everything we needed as a family more easily, but I still felt an overwhelming urge to pitch in and help. They refused all my money. It broke my heart and my guilt didn't subside; in fact, it grew.

Often the guilt would become so acute that it would create its own panic attack. Other times, the guilt would create a brand of anxiety that would infest my life and feed upon itself for years.

By this time, my father had started his own blow molding company called Luben Plastics. I would help out when I could and learned that I really liked working with my hands on the machines. And I really enjoyed working again with my father. In 1979, I graduated high school and immediately went to work full-time. It wasn't long before Jack, my father's right-hand man and loyal employee who had worked side-by-side with him for many years, suddenly quit. I always believed he saw my arrival as an insult -- he assumed I would be trained to take over the family business one day, and he saw his opportunity for advancement disappear. (I don't know why because I had only worked part-time.) At that point in my career, I had no idea what I was doing: I had never been in business for myself, I couldn't repair any of the blow molding machines, and I didn't know the first thing about sales except I knew that the salesmen were the guys who always wore nice suits and drove the fancy cars. But honestly, I couldn't see

My father working on one of his
blow molding machines.

ever driving off to some unknown place to meet with strangers and try to get them to buy something from me. Just the thought itself raised my anxiety to uncomfortable levels.

I always figured I would end up being a shop mechanic. I expected I would learn all about how the blow molding machines operated, I would figure out how to fix them, then someday I would become the shop supervisor. Of course I had dreams and aspirations of being rich someday, but I had no fathomable idea of how that could possibly happen. Maybe I could invent something, I would think to myself, then people would have to come see me and I could deal with them on my own turf where I felt safe, and I would avoid all the panic and the fear of having to travel to see them.

My father may never admit it, but I think he was really pissed that Jack left his company the way he did, and subconsciously, he transferred a little of that anger onto me. Jack's sudden departure created a lot more work, and my father had to shoulder nearly the entire workload himself. Being the guilt-master I am, I forced myself to work harder and harder, trying to learn as much as I could as fast as I could. Most, if not all that happens behind the scenes in a plastics blow molding company, is manual labor -- and that was something I could understand and do quickly to become useful. We did not have any of those fancy box making machines in our shop; instead, the boxes all had to be made by hand. I had to set up the box, put the bottles in the box, tape them up, then stack the boxes on skids. Being in great shape and fresh out of high school, I had a deep reserve of strength and energy, and I dove right in. My usual 9:00 to 5:00 shift become more like 7:30 to 6:30. And in such a competitive industry as plastics, the shop needed to run on a six or seven day week as a 24-hour operation. Every minute that the machines were down and not churning out new bottles, we were losing opportunities to make money.

Jack had been a very good mechanic and supervisor, and I was neither. But I would watch my father diligently, and though we did have fun together at times, most of the time my work life was filled with stress and deepening guilt. My father was a great mechanic in his own right, and had worked on these machines for years, but he didn't know everything about the newer machines he had purchased. The older machines in the shop were breaking down and gradually being replaced by newer models. And though the fancy new machines were more efficient, they included many solid state components that my father had never seen before.

So I took it upon myself to try my best to learn schematics, mechanics, pneumatic pressure on my own -- everything associated with running, operating and maintaining a modern blow molding machine. In my head, I had caused my father's right-hand man and mechanic to quit. I accepted that it was all my fault. I had screwed this up. So it was up to me to make sure nothing ever hindered these machines. No one asked me to, but I made it solely my responsibility. This developed my sense of urgency and heightened my anxiety.

I pride myself on being a hard worker. Everywhere I have ever worked, my bosses have said I did a great job -- and I'm confident I always did. I would always put in extra time and extra effort. Whether it was at the wiener joint, or at a gas station, or delivering newspapers, I always wanted to show that I was the guy who was going to give you that little extra. Maybe it was the guilt that drove me; I didn't want to let anybody down. I wondered sometimes if I even deserved my pay.

There are a thousand things that can go wrong with a blow molding machine, and I promise not to bore you with details about every one of them. But the bottom line is that if you have the right personnel in the right positions, mistakes and breakdowns can be limited. And we, unfortunately, did not. As a new company, we couldn't afford the best help, and in my opinion, many of the employees who worked our second and third shifts just didn't give a shit at all -- they would arrive, go through the motions, put in their time, punch out, and then go home, that is, if they happened to show up at all. As the new supervisor, I would stay in charge until the next supervisor arrived. Some nights, my relief would show up at 4:30, some nights 5:30, and some nights not at all. Some nights I would be stuck in the shop until midnight praying the third shift supervisor would come in. And many times, he didn't.

With all this time on my hands, I trained myself to become the head mechanic. I learned as much as I could on the job, and piled on new responsibilities. Now it was guaranteed that when anything went wrong, my anxiety, panic and guilt levels would ascend to astronomical levels. I would own every screw-up. Things couldn't ever go wrong or I would be letting my family down.

Back then, if I took a rare night off and went out on a date, I would carry a beeper. If the beeper went off in the middle of dinner or a movie -- and it frequently did – it meant something was wrong on the machine the supervisor could not fix and we would have to jump in the car and race back to the shop. It would have been easier if I had just called the shop and said I would address it first thing in the morning, but not me. Not Mr. Guilt. Instead I would go to work and leave my date (and future wife Robbie) sleeping in the car until it was time to take her home. I felt incredibly guilty doing that to her, it broke my heart, but I felt more guilty that by not being in the shop when I was needed, I was letting my family down. Then, after I took Robbie home, I would end up returning to the shop to finish up. This was not slave labor. No one was pointing a gun to my head. No one told me to do it. It was my choice. I took it upon myself because the guilt drove me to it.

Once when I was still in high school, I remember my father coming home one night late, exhausted, his blue overalls caked with grease. It killed me to see him look like that. The guilt was overwhelming and was the reason I went to work for him in the first place. I was a 17-year-old with a good head on my shoulders and I could have gone to college or done anything I wanted, for that matter. But I chose this life, and if I didn't like it, there was no one to blame for it but myself. In society today, everybody seems to like to point fingers when something doesn't go their way or they don't get what they want. There was only direction to point the finger -- at me. When you finally realize what agoraphobia is all about, you learn it's all up to you. You can choose to get better, or you will slowly sink into its depths.

My father had a head sales rep named Marco who was in charge of all our shop's sales. He was a cool, good-looking Italian guy with a great suit and a great car. He had confidence and swagger -- essentially, everything I wanted to have someday. I would pretend to walk around with that swagger, but it was just a show after all. What a joke. Deep down, I had no swagger. I was petrified of everything.

In the early 80's, Marco did something horrible and unforgivable. Behind my father's back, he established his own blow molding company. Essentially, he could now manufacture his own bottles and sell them to all the great accounts he had established while working for us.

I went crazy. I was absolutely furious! Here he was stealing from my father, taking the food right out of my family's mouths. A funny thing about anger fueled by guilt and anxiety -- it starts at level 9!

The moment I heard the news, I ran to my car and said I was going over to his new facility to straighten him out. It was the most angry I had ever been. My father could see the veins popping from my forehead and sensed what I was about to do, and he literally ran into the road and jumped in front of my car to stop me. I nearly ran him over.

It's important to note here that my anger here was two-fold. It wasn't just focused on my belief that he had ripped us off, it was also because I realized what was going to happen next. I would have to be the new salesman. I was too afraid to leave my own room and now I was going to have to learn and endure the whole list of those things that terrified me most. There was no greater insult. I hated Marco with every ounce of my soul for what he had just done to me.

I promised my father I would let it go, but I simply couldn't. The next day, I drove over to Marco's facility anyway, got up in his face, and told him in no uncertain terms that if he stole another piece of the business from my family, I would break his neck. And I meant it, too. I didn't care about the outcomes or ramifications; I was just too incensed.

As you can imagine, over the next several months, our order board became shorter and shorter as our accounts were instead filled by our new competitor, Marco. My mother and father pretended not to show it, but I could tell they were nervous about all our futures. But my parents have always been able to live in the moment better than I. I lived with anxiety in the future. I could not sleep at night because I was a complete mess, and because I knew they were worried, too. After long sleepless nights and long arguments with my inner demons, I decided I had to try it. I had to try to learn how to become a salesman. The guilt was driving me again. And I would endure it all without telling anybody.

Sales at the shop were slowly rebounding and were trickling in, but we were suddenly faced with another unforeseen crisis – the oil embargo. Because of the embargo, we were forced to pay cash in advance for all our new plastics material, which left the company with a zero cash flow. Money became extremely tight, tighter than it had ever been. I would work second and sometimes third shifts at the shop, go home to catch a few hours of sleep, slip on a suit, then go out and battle through panic attacks while trying to sell. My father would remain at the shop trying to keep the machines running without me, but over time, he couldn't keep up and it was taking its toll on him and the business.

My family business and my father were failing, and here I was, too handcuffed by anxiety and fear to walk into someone's office and ask for a simple order that would save us all -- my level of guilt about this had risen off the charts and was practically insurmountable. I would find myself parked on the side of the highway playing the *Theme to Rocky* over and over again just to build up enough nerve to drive over the damned George Washington Bridge. My throat would be closed, I would feel dizzy, and water would be cascading from my eyes and staining my shirt. Many times I would take the next available exit and head for home, fabricating some foolish story about how the customer just didn't want to buy from us today, or that they cancelled the appointment. The voices in my head were never more at odds -- one side telling me I was worthless and needed to turn north and go back home, while on the other side, the voices were urging me to continue to head south and fight, fight, fight for my family. I had no idea how to deal with this rollercoaster of emotions at the time, and it scared me shitless.

And I think what made it worse was that I knew I was becoming a great communicator. I was learning to sell! I enjoyed it, and I was damned good at it. My problem was never about convincing a customer to place the order, it was about just being able to get myself in front of that customer in the first place! If only I could have figured that son of a bitch out! I cried more times on the Connecticut Thruway than I can count. I sat hyperventilating in more hospital parking lots at this time than at any other time in my life. I would often find myself in full-fledged panic mode, cruising through supermarket parking lots praying for some sort of human interaction, approaching random strangers and creating conversations to calm myself down. I'm sure they thought I was completely insane. God forbid if they would ask if I was OK -- because it was so much worse if they noticed!

The business was failing, and we started to sell off our assets. It was ugly. My dad and I had always been the best of friends until we went to work together. Our relationship became strained not because we still didn't love each other, but because of the toll all this pressure had placed on both of us. I admit now that today, I am happy that Luben Plastics went out of business. I think it was for the best. My father, my mother and my brother were all deeply involved in the company and in its demise, and even today, our relationships continue to be strained from that terrible experience.

By 1989, I had opened a small gym, Champion Sports Gym. Working out had become a very important part of my life. We had to close the shop each year for a week to give employees with tenure vacation time. Between the pressure of the business and fighting to stay afloat, my anxiety tree's branches had now grown tentacles and they were reaching down to wrap themselves around my throat. To make matters worse, I learned when I returned to work that a new Gold's Gym would be opening just two miles from my own gym -- and this unexpected new competitor happened to be an old friend.

I worked for my father from 1979 until 1991 when the company finally collapsed.

Looking back on it now, I can't blame Marco. After all, he did exactly what my father had done -- left a good company to start his own. That's simple capitalism at work -- it's the American Dream -- and there's nothing wrong with doing that. I had considered that guy who opened the competing gym to be a friend -- in fact, he was even at my wedding! But again, that's capitalism. That's business. And that can be good.

Back then, guilt, fear, anxiety and panic filled my days, drove me, and enslaved me into an industry and a way of life.

Oh, and to update you all... I heard that the friend of mine who started the gym has found himself up to his eyeballs in legal problems now, and we learned Marco went of business just three years after he left us.

But that's capitalism at work, too. I don't feel guilty about that.

9

SUCCESS

The difference between a successful person and others is not a lack of strength, not a lack of knowledge, but rather a lack of will.

~ Vince Lombardi

Every person defines success a different way; it can mean anything to anybody.

For some, success might mean attaining world-wide fame. For others, success could mean receiving critical acclaim for their original art work, or reaching distinction at the top of their chosen field. And for some, success is measured in the form of wealth and large financial rewards.

For many others, success is defined more humbly. It could mean making the team, getting a new job, or securing a great promotion. Or it could mean falling in love, raising a family, or just leading a simple, quiet, happy life.

And sometimes, especially for those of us afflicted with anxiety and panic attacks, success comes measured in moment-to-moment doses, too. *Can I get over that bridge? Will I make it up this elevator? Can I get through this meeting?* It doesn't seem fair to have to fight with one hand tied behind your back, but it is important to know that no matter how severe the attacks may be, every kind of success you could dream of is still very possible.

But whether afflicted or not, unless you're born with the vocal cords of Frank Sinatra or can throw a fastball with precision at 95 miles per hour, you're probably like me and will have to go to work to earn the money you need to make those dreams come true.

I don't believe that the old saying, *"find something you love and you'll never have to work a day in your life"* to be the best advice. In my opinion, it's better to find something you can make money at, then go off and do those things that you love to do. I didn't wake up one morning thinking, *"Hey I have a great idea! Why don't I become a multi-millionaire selling empty plastic bottles!"* For me, success came when I simply recognized an opportunity.

Over the years, while battling anxiety and panic, I was able to build a plastics packaging company from scratch that turned ten and fifteen cent items into over $20 million in sales. We're not selling $250,000 Lamborghinis or $3 million yachts here either, we've achieved our success -- *literally* -- fifteen cents at a time.

It took years of getting my ass kicked while trying to get my foot in the door of customers who did not want to see me, and all the while, dealing with horrible bouts of anxiety and panic. When I first started, suppliers literally laughed in my face; they just couldn't figure out how a kid in his twenties could possibly survive in the business. Why should they sell their empty containers to me if they could just as easily sell them to someone or some company that was more established?

My company, Ocean State Packaging, is all about sales. I believe that selling is the hardest and most important job in any business. I'm not talking here about the clerk at your local store who might sell you a washing machine, a pair of shoes, or a candy bar across a counter. I'm talking about the professional salesperson who needs to cold call a potential new customer hundreds of miles away, then try to establish a relationship with that customer while battling over 1,200 other hard-nosed competitors. Sometimes it would take as many as five to ten visits or more, driving or flying, over the course of months, only to be turned away with a handshake or the passing of a business card... *thanks for coming in, maybe next time? See you in a few weeks?* This is real selling -- get to know your customer in a very short period of time, get them to like you, get them to trust you, and finally get them to try your product and then buy it from you.

Yet I do not consider myself a salesman, and I never refer to my sales staff as salesmen either. To me, good salespeople are relationship people just as I am, but in real life I'm a dad, a husband, a baseball coach and a lot of other things, too. And I recognize those characteristics in all our staff as we expect them to recognize those same traits in our clients.

At the time there were over 1,500 blow molding companies in North America, and there were over 2,000 plastic brokers and distributors that we had to compete with every day. I love to brag that Ocean State Packaging is one of the premier plastic packaging companies in the country. Many of our clients are second, third and fourth generation customers -- a fact unheard of in this business that is well known for an astronomical turnover rate. I need to mention that bringing in my brother Stephen as well as Bryan Plotts, who is also considered family, has been the turning point at Ocean State Packaging and a tribute to its rise and continued success. I love this company and I feel a great source of personal pride in it.

My road to success while building this company and dealing with anxiety and panic has been long and arduous, but I accepted that if I had any hope of success in my life, I needed to do three things better than anyone. First, I needed to listen and trust very smart people. Second, I needed to study how to make my limited resources work for me through commercial real estate, stocks, bonds and other investment vehicles. And third, I needed to read, read, and read some more.

I did not attend college; instead, I chose to study at the school of the real world where success isn't measured by a diploma or plaque hanging on an office wall, but by how big the number is at the bottom of a company's balance sheet. It is not my intent to downplay formal higher education here, but it just wasn't my path. When you need a brain surgeon, you'd better believe that their education, master's degree, doctorate, residency program and reputation are critical to your decision and treatment. But I don't deal with life and death in my world; success here is measured by nothing other than how large that black number is on the bottom line.

Understand, too, that it is hard enough for me to talk about my anxiety, never mind talk about my financial success. It feels unnatural. But to understand me and what I have endured, I accept that it's important also to understand where I've landed. I have built a successful business that has given me boats, cars, vacation homes, and all the wonderful freedoms that money can bring to anyone. But more important than that, I have two incredible kids and a loving wife without whose strength and support I wouldn't have achieved a thing, even though she was blind to the chaos I was going through. (And I know it still pains her to read about it now.) Our company also employs hundreds of people who rely on the income we generate to support their own families, husbands, wives, and children and I consider that a big part of our success, too.

Most readers have likely never heard of Ocean State Packaging, and that's OK. But millions have seen and used our bottles at auto dealerships, hospitals, hairdressers, restaurants, pharmacies, drug stores, gas stations, all the major retail and wholesale chains, and in many of the best hotels in the world.

Today, when I walk into a random store somewhere and happen to notice one of our bottles on a shelf, I smile as I always remember the story behind it. And there really is a story behind every one of them, I promise. Some of these stories have me running in panic out of the waiting room, or listening to the *Theme from Rocky* while trying to build up the motivation and momentum I needed to simply survive a fifteen-minute conversation with another human being.

Just a sample of the plastic bottles that Ocean State Packaging distributes. You might recognize a few of them just from their shape.

If you happen to suffer from anxiety and panic attacks, I invite you to lay your own stories of fear and embarrassment over mine. Perhaps my stories can serve as a template in some way. Then use my thoughts and achievements to help you realize that you don't need to live that way, that success is possible, that there is a way out, and that fighting yourself is not the answer.

Growing up and working in my father's struggling company I dreamed I would be a millionaire someday. I could even visualize myself on a yacht cruising across Narragansett Bay on a warm summer afternoon. Personally, I find it difficult to believe anyone who tells me they don't want to be a millionaire. If you were offered a million dollar paycheck every year for the rest of your life, would you really be eager to turn that down? Looking back, of course I would have loved to have had someone just hand me the money so that I wouldn't have had to worry. But that didn't happen, and I had no safety net below me to lessen my anxiety and break my fall. As I write this, sitting outside a building that I own, I can look up and say with confidence that I made this -- I did not inherit it. There is tremendous satisfaction in knowing that. You will never hear me blame anyone for the bad things that have happened in my life. Good or bad, it was my life. I chose the path. I made the mistakes. I chose to become wealthy. I chose to outwork everybody. I chose to overcome the anxiety and panic.

So I choose to define success, for the purposes of this book, to be about achievement, financial security and freedom. That doesn't mean I don't recognize and appreciate the many other successes I've experienced along the way. Signing every new customer was a success, every good grade my kids brought home was a success, every victory on the ball field was a success, every family vacation was a success, and on and on.

There is a line in the Michael Douglas movie *Wall Street* that says, *"the point is, ladies and gentlemen, that greed, for lack of a better word, is good."* Well, as long as you don't hurt someone, on some level, I tend to agree with that. There is nothing wrong with *wanting* -- we all want something. Greed is similar to ego. As long as you learn and understand which part of your ego is good, and which part isn't (like sorting out good habits from bad habits), it will work in your favor. Wanting a good thing badly enough can be a powerful and constructive motivator.

Once you learn what anxiety and panic attacks are and how to use them to your advantage, you will no longer fear the next job interview, you will no longer fear the next opportunity, and you will no longer fear taking risks like starting your own business.

As I often say, anxiety lives in the future, not the present. The only thing stopping you from achievement is <u>not</u> you -- *it's your thoughts*! I can only imagine what I would have accomplished over the course of the last 35 years without carrying around the baggage of these crippling panic attacks. Again, I'm in no way saying *"woe is me."* It's just the way it was. I now accept that.

I am blessed and grateful to be living the life I've always dreamed about. It reminds me of the REO Speedwagon song *Live Every Moment* that I used to play over and over and over for motivation.

> *Live every moment -- love every day*
> *'Cause if you don't, you might just throw your love away.*

The song was a little motivational pill I would use back in the 80's. God, I wish the effect didn't wear off just a few minutes after the song ended, though. Because after the endorphins died down, I would retreat back to that scary place in my thoughts again.

But now I'm here to tell you I made it through to the other side, even with one hand tied behind my back.

And all this from a company started in a bedroom by a guy too terrified to leave it.

10

THE BUSINESS CONFERENCE

There are nights when the wolves are silent and only the moon howls.

~ George Carlin

There are certain words you should never use around someone who has agoraphobia, and they include *vacation, trip, journey,* and *travel.* Mere mention of these terms can send them into a fit of terror.

Embarking on any kind of trip means abandoning your safe place and leaving behind everything that you know best and those things that keep your anxiety in check. Even if you do not know what's wrong with you, you find immense comfort knowing there is help just around the corner if you ever need it. Travelling to an unknown destination throws that security to the wind.

And the only other word I can think of that might be worse than *trip* is *conference*.

I have missed out on countless business trips over the years due to my condition. I always tried to make excuses, create an illness or flat-out lie to avoid every kind of travel. But there were also those times when there was nothing I could do. I had to take the trip -- *I had to do it anyway.*

In the plastics industry, I made my reputation as a middleman connecting vendors who manufacture the product with new customers who need it. It may sound counterintuitive, but in this business, vendors are always more important than customers. I believed with a little hustle, I could always find a new customer, but there really are only a limited number of important vendors. After all, without product, there is no business anyway.

Because of this, when I first started my company, the stress that accompanied keeping our vendors happy was extreme. Early on, I was lucky to become friendly with a large bottle cap company in New Jersey. I did everything I could to grow our business relationship, and by all accounts, I was succeeding. In fact I was so successful, I was personally invited to attend their "conference" -- a ski trip business getaway to beautiful Vermont.

The truth was that this was my second invitation; I had successfully excused myself the year before, avoiding the trip. But now this vendor had become even more important to my bottom line and was supplying eleven of my best customers. I was worried about everything. I couldn't do anything that might insult them. I could not risk jeopardizing our relationship.

My contact with this vendor was their sales manager. He was a complete jerk and well-known to treat people like shit. But I needed him, and I was able to get into his good graces so well that he invited me along on this wonderful trip. Other invitees included over 120 other people who were also their customers. And because I was a bottle distributor, they wanted me there badly -- we were in short supply. I knew they needed me to be there, but I couldn't let on that I needed them more.

The resort was only about five hours from my office, so like every good agoraphobic, I left at 11 o'clock in the morning to ensure I would arrive safely several hours early. I could not deal with the idea of getting lost, and I absolutely couldn't handle driving alone after dark. As you might expect, I was the first to arrive at the facility and was so early my room wasn't even ready yet. So what do you do when you're in Vermont with nothing else to do? You drive around until you find the nearest hospital, of course. And I found it eight miles away.

Now I had to endure the weekend taming a two-headed monster. In addition to handling the problems associated with my usual anxiety issues, I had a very important vendor I had to impress and keep happy. What made it worse was when I realized that nine of my regular customers were going to be there, too. This conference had rapidly developed into an agoraphobic's worst nightmare.

We all stayed in a series of cabins that most people would consider quite charming, but I considered complete hell. There were no televisions or radios, and the only saving grace was an open bar that was available to us every night. I also learned that each of these small cabins would house twelve of us. I found it weird that I'd be sharing a bathroom with a dozen people I didn't even know. And these weren't just any people: the guest list for this conference and trip included several high-profile executives running public companies, CEO's, and CFO's. In fact, they could all potentially become new customers of mine someday.

And of course there was little me, the owner of a company called Ocean State Packaging, a guy scared to leave his house, scared to ride a ski lift, and scared of just about everything. I had to not only act like nothing was bothering me, but at the same time, I had to act like I belonged with this crowd and spend my time trolling for new customers. To a salesperson, it was a veritable buffet of new business. But the only goal I could focus on was to simply make it through the first night.

After we all took our turns bellying up to the open bar, everyone was introduced and somebody stood up and gave a small speech. I left the room to fake a call so I didn't have to speak. Then the guy said, "OK everybody, let's get to bed early. We're meeting for breakfast at 5:45 and then taking the buses up to the mountain!" Everyone applauded.

The last thing in the world I wanted to do was go to bed early. I did not want to be alone in a strange place in the dark with just my thoughts to guide me. Everyone shook hands, exchanged a few friendly hugs, and dispersed. I crawled off to find my numbered room and sit in the dark. I knew I wouldn't sleep.

The only good thing about my room was it was full of books. I had never heard of most of the titles, but the selection included a copy of *Moby Dick*. It didn't take long before I could hear snoring through the thin cabin wall behind me. How dare they sleep! Just like on the gondola, and on the airplane, I hated them. These guys were pulling in salaries in the hundreds of thousands of dollars, having a good time, and I hated them all. I opened *Moby Dick* to a random chapter and started to read. I read the same chapter at least a dozen times. To this day, I still have no recollection of what it said.

As the night grew later, the fear inside me grew darker right along with it. I felt like a caged animal. I had many hours to reflect, and at some point in the midst of the torture, I rebelled.

Fuck this. I am going to figure this out. I am not going to go insane here. I am going to work through this.

When you're getting ready to work out, or getting ready to fight, there is an adrenaline rush. There is a moment when you realize that the battle is you against you -- some refer to this as "the fight in you." I have always had an aggressive side to me, and it's great to draw on when you're trying to pick a fight in a bar, but it sucks like hell when you're trying to relax and fall asleep at night.

It's at night when the fear and anxiety do their best job of seeping in. And every time I tried to fight it, the bad thought process would reboot itself and start all over again. The tentacles of fear and doubt grow, become stronger, and try to drive me insane. The cycle was vicious. And after just five more hours of this, I knew I had no choice but to get up and go on a bunch of gondola rides with these guys.

I made it through the weekend the same way I made it through most trips in my life -- with fake smiles, alcohol, and bits of sleep only when the sun started to rise. Some nights were better, and some nights were worse, but no night was free of it all.

There were many plastics conventions and conferences that I attended through the years. I would not sleep in the days leading up to them, and sometimes not for weeks before. I would be anxious about the plane rides, the tunnels, the accommodations... everything. There was one time when I was sitting on a small shuttle plane in Providence waiting to leave for New York where I would need to transfer and take another flight to Chicago. I was in the middle of a level 9 panic attack, and I guess I just didn't have the fight in me that day. Just before the door closed, I hopped up and bolted off. This lead to another ride in the back of a police car. It was a challenge to try to explain to the police what I was feeling without convincing them I was insane. I insisted I was just sick and needed to get off and get some air. No big deal.

I'm saddened by all the time I've lost. I'm amazed by how much time I wasted from my late teens into my twenties and into my thirties. It makes me sick to think of what I could have accomplished if I had used all that energy productively.

I mention early in this book that I never wanted to write about these things. That's true. These chapters are as real now as I write them as they were when they happened. And I can feel the anxiety rise in my core as I relive so many of these awful moments. It's incredible how powerful the feelings were and how I can still feel them all these years later. I wrote that this book will open old wounds that have scabbed over. That's not a pretty image or easy to do. But I still maintain that this story needs to be told and will help people. People need to hear this story and laugh, cry, and be embarrassed right along with me because they need to know that you can not only survive this, you can live, thrive, and prosper. You can be happy. I can say that I have been both cursed and blessed with this thing, and despite the viciousness of it all, it has made me stronger. And it's only now that I can admit and appreciate that.

For those afflicted, maybe this book will give you the mental strength to go back and visit those people who you pretended were not there or live so far away. If you are in business, maybe it will give you the strength to visit your own vendors and customers you thought were too big or unreachable. It's what I did, and as I look back on it now, I am glad I did it anyway.

The fear of death is more dreaded than death itself.
~ Publilius Syrus

11

THE WEDDING

Always and forever; each moment with you. Is just like a dream to me;
that somehow came true. And I know tomorrow; will still be the same.
Cause we've got a life of love; that won't ever change.

~ Heatwave

I had started to drink at around 10 o'clock that morning.
And now as I look back at my wedding day pictures from thirty
years ago, in almost every one, there I am holding a bottle of
beer. But hey, it was my wedding day after all, and it was easy to
convince myself and my friends that I was drinking to celebrate and
have a great time. But deep down, I had decided I needed that

alcohol to suppress my anxiety. I believed I had no choice. I knew what was coming. I needed to find a way to survive that day. A funny thing about alcohol though: no matter how much of it you drink, the anxiety always seems to remain, inviting you to drink just a little bit more.

My wife Robbie was, and still is, the most beautiful person both inside and out I have ever known. I credit my success to her, and there is no doubt that if not for her love and support, today I would be in some awful, unthinkable place. Any rational person would have been looking forward to this moment -- to be 25 years old and have an opportunity to wed the most beautiful woman on the planet, then jet off together for a romantic honeymoon in the Caribbean paradise of Antigua. Could a man be any more fortunate?

But for me, there was little joy. For better than a month leading up to the wedding, I had been an absolute mess.

Our wedding day, 1986.

People afflicted with anxiety and panic disorders cannot stomach the thought of having attention fixed on them. And when that attention comes from the eyes of hundreds of family members and friends, people who know you well, all sitting silently in rows, all with their thoughts fixed directly on you, that pain is magnified. The anxiety growing in my mind was building itself up to astronomical levels. If I wasn't sure I would be able to utter "I do," then how the hell could I expect myself to make it through an hour-long ceremony?

The "what ifs" became unending --

What if my throat starts to close? What if I can't breathe? What if I have a heart attack? What if I pass out in front of my bride, my family, and all my friends? What if I end up lying on the floor for all to see, right in the middle of the church? I can't possibly make excuses for this one. I can't fake being sick. What if my bride's family sees me panic, lose control, humiliate myself and run as fast as I can up the aisle and straight out of that church? How can I do this to the woman I love so deeply? What kind of complete ass am I?

My brother Steve served as my best man that day, and we had started drinking together at home. Robbie and I had scheduled an afternoon ceremony, and by the time I arrived, I estimate I had already consumed over fifteen beers. I remember sitting in the back of the limo heading for the church drinking as much as I could, wishing the limo would slow down so I could drink a little more.

I recall standing on the church steps greeting my family and all my great friends as they arrived, inebriated, doing everything in my power to appear happy, yet all the while I was scared shitless, babbling to myself. *You can do this, Brian. Suck it up. Deal with it. Pull yourself together. Fuck, just do it. What the hell is wrong with you?* And all the while I had one of those little devils standing on my shoulder shouting into my ear. *You're weak. You're afraid. You're going insane. You're going to have a heart attack. They're all going to laugh at you. You are going to humiliate yourself.*

People who suffer from anxiety and panic attacks understand this all too well. There is one part of your being always fighting and in conflict with another part of your being. Talking to yourself becomes the norm. Essentially, my egos were working against each other. Little did I know then that dealing with these egos, not ignoring them, would play an important role in my future healing process.

But for now, the problem at hand was figuring out how to fake it and walk into that church looking like I was the most confident, cool, collected husband any gal could ever hope to marry.

As alcohol leaves your system, it leaves behind a void that causes your anxiety levels to ramp up higher and faster as your adrenaline takes over. It had been at least an hour since I was able to get access to a drink, and now the effects of the alcohol were wearing off just as we arrived at the altar and our priest told the congregation to take their seats. I felt my anxiety spike.

Today, I admit that my memory of those moments is not too good and sadly enough, the parts I do recall are those moments when I was wrapped up in the worst of the fears. However, I do remember kneeling at the altar, and I remember glancing over at Robbie -- she looked radiant dressed in white. Absolutely perfect! She looked back at me and I thank God she couldn't read my mind at that precise moment. The absolute terror I felt had nothing to do with a fear of marriage -- I wanted to marry her more than anything I have ever wanted in this world; it had everything to do with my physical and mental responses -- problems that I could have controlled (and more importantly dealt with) if I had known what the hell was wrong with me in the first place. And more importantly, how to deal with it.

For me, time in that church had come to a virtual standstill. Our forty-five minute wedding ceremony felt like it lasted about five hours. I could almost feel every second click off the clock. But when the moment arrived to read our vows, I was surprised to feel my anxiety ease ever so slightly -- from level 8 down to level 7 -- because I realized that we were almost done. The end of the ceremony was near. I considered that maybe if I had made it this far without losing control, I could make it just a little further.

Today, Robbie knows the details of my day very well, and I know she feels horrible because I didn't tell her what I was going through. *Fight, fight, fight* -- what a terrible way to go through life. Oh, how I wish I knew then what I know today.

"Hey Brian... you're having an anxiety attack. So, just do this... and this... and that... and it will all be just fine. And by the way... congratulations!"

Mercifully, the ceremony ended and we walked straight back up the aisle and out of the church onto the front steps. I swear to God that it was one of the most wonderful feelings of my life not only because I had just married my childhood sweetheart, but because that horrible wedding experience was over. I know Robbie now understands and has accepted how I felt that day, but it still hurts me terribly to write about it even thirty years later. I still wish to God there was some way I could go back and explain to that poor guy what he could have done.

So I had somehow survived the wedding -- on to the reception!

For everyone, a reception is all about food, dancing, drinking, music and fun -- that is, except for me. You see, my head was positioned firmly in the future; that's where anxiety lives and does its damndest to control you. While everybody was having a great time, my mind was off somewhere else lost in worry. In a few days, I would be boarding a plane where I would be trapped for six hours on our trip to Antigua -- *son of a bitch.*

I did my best to forget I was soon leaving on a honeymoon, and instead, tried to just enjoy the atmosphere and live inside the moment. Everyone I knew was here just like they were at the wedding, but not everyone's focus was on me -- they were all darting around talking, drinking, visiting with each other and having a perfectly good time. It's exactly what I needed them to do. My anxiety dropped all the way to level 1.

But each time I felt myself start to relax and have fun, some well-meaning guest always seemed to show up to throw their arm across my shoulders and ask, "*Wow, Brian, Antigua! You ready for that honeymoon?*" I wanted to tell them to shut the hell up and plead with them to please let me enjoy at least a few moments of relative calm. It's funny how that works. People want to live in the moment, but no one really ever does. People always tend to think a day, a week, or a year in advance. Creating ways to think in the present is another critical component to control severe anxiety.

Robbie worked as a flight attendant and had flown in more planes than most folks had ridden bicycles. She didn't have any fear of flying at all. For me though, six hours trapped and belted inside an aluminum tube at 35,000 feet equaled anxiety level 9. I couldn't believe there was anything worse.

Robbie knew I was not fond of flying, but she had no idea to what extent. I considered using every possible excuse to get out of that trip, but how on earth could I do that to her? I couldn't back out now. I couldn't show this beautiful newlywed how wimpy her new husband really was and that in truth, I was afraid of most everything in life -- not real things of course, but imagined things that were in my head. Things that were irrelevant. Things that were more horrifying than any experience I could encounter in reality. I am now reflecting back to the anxiety tree mentioned previously, that if left alone, it acts like a tree that continually grows roots. These roots grow deeper, and the tree becomes stronger and the leaves spread wide. The "what ifs" turn into the most horrible thoughts anchored by those roots and never leave you. How to prune that tree from a mighty tree down to a controlled little stump is so important to me now, but not something I could begin to fathom back then.

As I expected, my anxiety on our flight to Antigua was at level 9 the entire way. Realizing that the alcohol had heightened my anxiety at the wedding, I chose not to drink on the plane. I looked around the cabin at our fellow passengers and decided that I absolutely hated every one of them -- they were calm, relaxed, and many slept soundly. I glanced over at Robbie and realized she had fallen asleep, too, a victim of our very busy week. I was alone with no one to talk to, except of course, my own conflicted thoughts.

Believe it or not, I would call this experience the worst moment of my life. I was crawling out of my skin and felt myself losing control. What will happen if I really lose it this time, I wondered. Will I rush to the front of the plane, open the door and jump? Will I charge into the cockpit and demand the pilot land the plane and let me off? Will I run up and down the aisle screaming at the passengers like a mad raving lunatic? Maybe I will kill one of them with my bare hands?

I squeezed the armrest of my seat until my knuckles turned white as my anxiety level dropped from 9 to 7, then back to 9 then back to 7 then 9 -- all the way to Antigua. The best part of the trip was when I heard the plane's engines back off as we started our decent. I felt an instant drop in my anxiety level when I realized this horrifying ordeal was almost over, and I immediately fell asleep. The extreme emotional and physical exhaustion had taken its toll.

Most people who have a fear of flying fear crashing. But not me. When my anxiety level peaked at level 9, a crash was exactly what I prayed for. When I tell others about this reaction, they think I'm joking -- but I swear I am serious. I don't want to die; I just need relief from the perpetual torture. Think about the terror 200 passengers might suddenly feel if they thought their plane was about to crash. It's what I feel while we're cruising along calmly. I just might look around the plane and shout at them, *"There, you see? That's what I've been feeling since we took off!"*

Since then, I have flown hundreds of flights for thousands of miles and have developed tools and techniques to deal with my anxiety in the air. Flying may never become my favorite thing to do, but I now know how to keep my anxiety below a level 3 whenever I need to do it.

Once safely in Antigua, I disembarked the plane and ran to the first thing I saw -- beer! I have never been so dehydrated, exhausted, and exhilarated at the same time in my life. It might have been the most satisfying beer I have ever tasted. For five minutes, life was great.

And then I remembered that in 10 days, I had to get on that plane again to return home. So here I was in the Caribbean paradise of Antigua at the exclusive St. James Club, in an exotic tropical jungle, alone with the woman of my dreams, and I was a complete mess. But anxiety over our return trip was only part of the problem.

You might remember the book and movie *The Amityville Horror* from the late 70's. In the film, the lead character wakes up at precisely 3:15 every morning. At some point in high school I realized that I, too, wake at about 3:15 every morning and it really freaked me out when I saw this happen to that poor guy in the movie. But each time that I would wake, I found myself in the middle of my own personal horror -- my heart would be beating through my chest, my throat would be closing and I would be drenched in a soaking sweat. Many nights I dreaded going to sleep knowing I would wake up inside this terror with anxiety racing through my veins.

And sure enough, on the very first night of our honeymoon, it happened.

At precisely 3:15 a.m., I awoke in the midst of a full-blown panic attack. I needed to find a distraction right away. My first instinct was to reach for the remote and turn on the TV, but despite the elegance of the hotel, the room didn't have one. I ran out onto the balcony, but there I found only the serene, unfamiliar quiet of the nearby jungle. I ran to the bathroom to look for a book or magazine to read, but there wasn't a page to be found anywhere. I even turned on the radio, but the only station our room could receive didn't play music, but ironically, the DJ was reading the obituaries of people who had recently died on the island. As I recount that first night, it sounds like a bad comedy routine, but trust me on this, it was far from funny.

People who experience these nighttime attacks look forward to sunrise. They beg to see that shimmer of light appear out over the eastern horizon. Hyperventilating, I stared out from our room across the balcony into the black Caribbean sky, checking my swift pulse rate, feeling my heart pound, and then, a little after 5 a.m. as it does every day, the sky began to brighten. My anxiety instantly eased. I felt better, returned to bed and fell back to sleep.

My wife woke up a few hours later around 8:30, and I woke right along with her as if nothing unusual had happened at all. After we dressed and had breakfast, I found I was able to enjoy a little of our time at the resort, that is, until 5 p.m. came rolling around again and my anxiety started to build. After my wife went to sleep, I looked ahead at those hours with complete dread.

Until recently, Robbie had no idea that I repeated this insane routine every night for all ten nights of our honeymoon.

To say that I survived my honeymoon is both a sad and a profound understatement. I have been tormented by this crap half my life, and I hate that I haven't been able to enjoy those parts of my days that should have been the happiest. I wish I could go back and live all these moments over again, to enjoy what everyone else enjoys. I can't help feeling something has been stolen from me that cannot be replaced.

People who know me might question the veracity of these tales, and I must admit, at times they sometimes seem unbelievable even to me. But I lived them. And I know other people afflicted with panic and anxiety attacks will recognize parts of themselves weaved into these personal stories and, I hope, begin to realize they are not alone and there is help available if they want it. I wish today that I had been more honest with the people who cared for me back then, and wish I had been more aggressive pursuing consistent psychological help. But I still believe there is a good reason why I had these attacks. And I have to wonder if perhaps I have been placed on this earth to use my experiences to help other people who endure their own unchecked panic and anxiety.

I have learned that the more I am willing to reveal of myself, the more people will listen, and the more people are willing to listen, then the more I will be able to help them. And of all the impossible things I could wish for over the rest of my life, perhaps that is one wish I can hope to realize.

A moment of bliss in our tropical honeymoon paradise.

Being deeply loved by someone gives you strength,
while loving someone deeply gives you courage.

~ Lao Tzu

12

THE CHILDREN

It is easier to build strong children than to repair broken men.

~ Frederick Douglass

Back when my son Michael played Little League Baseball, he would be so excited to play that he would have his uniform on and be ready to go hours before the game. It reminded me a little... of me! I've always loved baseball.

He was a terrific youth ballplayer, too, and at just 10 years old, he often faced off against kids as old as 12. Two years might not sound like much of an age difference, but at that stage of physical development, it very much is, especially when that 12-year-old big kid is throwing a baseball at you at 65 miles per hour from 46 feet away. Anyone who has ever coached or watched baseball at this level would swear that some of those 12 year olds looked like they had to be at least 18! He was a good, hard-working player and deserved to be playing in the upper age group with these older kids. His mom and I were very proud.

But in just his second game, one of those big kids on the mound unleashed a 65 mile-per-hour fastball that hit him in the back. I cringed and felt his pain, as every parent can attest, more than he did. Bravely, he trotted down to first base, tears streaming down his face. We checked him over and other than a bit of a red mark, thankfully, he wasn't hurt at all. It turned out to be just a glancing blow.

But as someone who suffers from anxiety and panic attacks, I had a unique insight into where my son's tears might be coming from. I worried that he would have a problem next time he batted. No one knows more than I how pain can manifest itself as both a physical and mental entity.

A few innings later, he was waiting on deck to bat again but he wasn't wearing a helmet and didn't have a bat in his hands. I could read the concern on his face. I walked over to him from where I was coaching near first base and asked, "So Mike... are you going to hit?"

He didn't answer. He looked up at me and his tears returned. He was afraid of getting hurt again -- and understandably so. But I sensed his tears were coming from elsewhere, too -- the embarrassment of running away and the guilt for having let me, his friends, and his teammates down. In a small way, this is what anxiety and panic is all about. It's about taking a single, small fear and letting it grow and embed itself, developing into something bigger that becomes difficult to control. I knew he was not going to step back into that batter's box on his own.

"Look," I said as a dad still struggling to find his own tools to deal with anxiety, "if you don't want to bat anymore, that's OK. Everyone will understand. But I also know that when you get home later, you'll be more upset. You'll be angry at yourself. And it will hurt even worse. Trust me."

I could see him rolling my comments over in his mind. He was torn. Give into the fear and go home, or step up to the plate and face it. I needed to give him a tool to guide him through this.

"I have an idea. What if you step up to the plate to hit, but just don't swing. Stand in the batter's box with the bat on your shoulder and let the pitcher throw it by you. Just go through the motions. No pressure. And do you know what? If you try it, I think you'll feel better about yourself later."

Mike

My son put on his helmet and stepped into the box. He trusted me, but I'm not sure how much he believed me, and I could see his hands were trembling. The big pitcher wound up and threw a fastball right by him for a strike as he lunged backwards. He took a deep breath, squeezed the bat a little tighter, and stepped back in for the second pitch. This time he didn't budge when it flew by.

Another fastball. Strike two. I swear I could see the relief melt off him.

Everyone has their own little story about facing a fear, like the old maxim about falling off a horse and getting right back on. Nipping a fear in the bud, head-on, when it is small and manageable, before it's allowed to germinate, is a great life lesson. When the pitcher's third pitch reached the plate, Michael swung and ripped a double to left field. His fear was gone. He was ecstatic. Compare that feeling to the feeling he would have had sitting at home in a self-destructive cloud of fear, anger, guilt, and embarrassment.

To this day while playing college ball, after he gets a hit, he'll look for me in the stands and touch his heart. And I'll touch my heart right back as I did that day.

* * * *

My daughter Jenn was an exceptional youth soccer player, but very shy. (Could she be like me, too?) The league's coaches were always on the lookout for the better, smarter players to help serve as game referees, and when she was asked, she was flattered and quite excited to try it.

But when we arrived at the field for her first game as an official, the reality set in that she would be overseeing girls two or three years older than she was, including many of her friends. Here she was, all dressed in her yellow uniform and ready to go to work, even with her own brand-new whistle dangling around her neck, yet she was starting to cry as we walked together toward the field.

"I'm so afraid," she confided.

So being the kind of father who was too afraid to ride an elevator or drive over a bridge, I had to find some tool or technique to help guide her through this.

"Listen," I began, "you know more about soccer than anyone else on the field today. That's why they asked you. You know you can do this."

"What if I make a bad call? What if my friends hate me? What if...?"

Jenn

What if? And where have I heard "what if" before!

"What if," I answered, "you just go out on the field and run around. Don't think of yourself as being in charge, just make believe you are one of the players. Let the other referee make all the calls. I'll bet that after you run around a little bit, you'll feel more comfortable. In fact, don't feel like you need to blow your whistle today at all."

She was still nervous, but it helped by knowing she had my support. I believed she felt most at home on the soccer field, and I think for her, it was a haven where she felt comfortable and safe. And just as I hoped and expected, the game started and after a few minutes, Jenn took control. She did a great job.

Jenn played in college and when she scored, I always touched my heart. That smile, no matter at 10 or 20, will never leave me.

Everyone wants their children to grow to be strong, confident and successful. But when teens don't have the tools to fix their own problems, they will often turn to alcohol and drugs. It's so much harder to learn problem-solving later in life.

For me, agoraphobia has been an indescribable curse. But sometimes, my experiences with it provide a rare blessing when it allows me to teach my kids how to deal with problems without fighting them.

13

THE PLACES OF ANXIETY

Far better is it to dare mighty things, to win glorious triumphs, even though checkered by failure... than to rank with those poor spirits who neither enjoy nor suffer much, because they live in a gray twilight that knows not victory nor defeat.

~ Theodore Roosevelt

I've discussed several common places that trigger episodes of anxiety in me, including bridges, tunnels, and airplanes. But these places are representative and I think of them as almost cliché, since whenever a movie or TV show portrays someone experiencing a panic attack, it is sure to feature one of these stereotypical locations.

The truth is that panic can be brought on by far more ordinary places and activities, and can even by prompted in places nearly everyone else finds relaxing, enjoyable, and even fun.

Our first vacation on a real cruise ship brought me all sorts of stress and anxiety, as you could probably imagine. Almost immediately after embarking, I wandered off without anyone knowing to locate the ship's infirmary. And then later that night at the first opportunity, I feigned a bad headache so I could visit the medical staff and interrogate them, all the while scanning their faces for reactions to my questioning. Sometimes you don't ask the questions when you know you won't like the answers. You work to fool yourself into believing what you want the answers to be. *What happens if someone gets really sick? What if someone has a heart attack? How do you get them off the ship? Does the Coast Guard come and get you?* But this time, their answers reassured me. I doubt I would have made it through the trip any other way.

Popular places like Disneyworld and Epcot, resorts that offer unparalleled family fun to millions, scare the shit out of me. With mammoth-sized parks and visitors that number in the thousands, unexpected, irrational anxiety lurks around every corner. And just when I'd begin to get my anxiety under control, down to maybe a 4 or 5, I would be greeted by a sign:

"WARNING! FOR SAFETY, YOU SHOULD BE IN GOOD HEALTH AND FREE FROM HIGH BLOOD PRESSURE, HEART, BACK, OR NECK PROBLEMS, MOTION SICKNESS, OR OTHER CONDITIONS THAT COULD BE AGGRAVATED BY THIS ADVENTURE."

Gee, Walt, thanks for the reminder.

Though to be honest, I found all those slow, silly, kiddie rides to be worse than the bigger, high-profile attractions. These rides would typically take place in some sort of boat that would float along leisurely though a dark tunnel to teach you about dinosaurs, your primitive ancestors, or feature singing dolls or songs about pirates. I would spend the entire ride scanning the walls for dimly-lit exit signs, and if I started to feel the anxiety rise in my chest, I would do my best to ignore the entertainment around me and instead focus on the glowing faces of my wife and kids. My only goal was to make it all the way to the end of the ride without humiliating myself or my family.

When my kids were young, I used to both love and hate taking them to the zoo. Zoos tend to be fun but organized with a maze of paths that all seem to lead to snack bars and gift shops, but almost never to medical help or the exits. I would be holding my kids by the hands following these confusing paths wondering... What's the fastest way out of here? What if I pass out and hit my head? My kids are so small; will they know what to do?

What if... What if... What if...

I learned to despise the word "vacation." I would become physically ill days before we'd be ready to leave to go anywhere. For days, my mind would roll through a list of all my sources of anxiety -- the flight, the cruise ship, an island hideaway, a hotel with elevators, nearby hospitals. Simply coping with vacation became a full-time activity. Sometimes in the middle of the night, I'd crawl out of bed and call down to the front desk of the hotel just to make sure somebody would be there to answer. And since in the middle of a full-fledged panic attack I wouldn't be able to get into an elevator, I would always ask for a room on the lower floors and then still map out all the staircases and exits. If we ended up staying on a higher floor, I would often raid the room's mini-bar for a few drinks to work up the nerve just to survive the elevator ride back down to the lobby.

It is always these little things that tend to bother me the most because in the mind of an agoraphobic, you're continually wondering how you could possibly handle all the big important things in life if you are distracted by all these little ones. Anxiety and panic are like the roots of a tree, and the longer you allow them to exist unchecked, the deeper those roots will extend into the fertile recesses of your mind.

To me, these roots represent not only fear but also the fear of the thought process itself. These fears may be irrational, but they are fears nonetheless. And as I've already mentioned, imagined fears tend to be far more acute and terrifying than those that come from real-life sources. People who are not afflicted with this disorder would be amazed at the terrors I am able to conjure. As the roots tunnel deeper, the branches of the anxiety tree grow higher, and the insecurities fracture and multiply into dozens of these "little things" -- going to the zoo, meeting a customer, riding an elevator -- that over time invade, control, and dominate every moment of your life.

I can't imagine where I would be today if I hadn't lived through this anxiety and panic. Would I have been more successful? Or maybe I wouldn't have been successful at all? There is no way to know, of course, but I do know that I didn't make peace with these daily little things until I learned not to fight them. It was the fighting that watered the tree and grew those roots.

Once, I had many places of anxiety. But now I am in a much better place.

14

QUIET THE MIND

I hear the waves
Sun beatin' down on my shoulders
It's a near-perfect day
Wishin' I wouldn't get any older
They say that it's gone 'fore you know it now

Quiet your mind
Soak it all in
It's a game you can't win
Enjoy the ride

~Zac Brown Band, *"Quiet Your Mind"*

So far in this book, I've discussed who I am, my family, and what I've accomplished in my life both professionally and financially.

These achievements are where I uncover some of my deepest joy and pride. But there is something more.

I am now able to take my 40-foot Azimut, *Jenny Girl*, ten to fifteen miles off shore and shut off the motor without any fear. I often sit there all afternoon alone, reading, writing, or sometimes just reflecting on how lucky I am. And hopefully while out there, I won't encounter another boat for hours. There was a time when I couldn't even comprehend that a day like this would be possible, never mind that I would actually enjoy something like this without any fear or worry.

And now I travel successfully all over the country building my company, contracting vendors, and meeting many great customers. They all see and know the real Brian now -- not the scared, worried, petrified Brian from before. I still lift weights and work out every single day and I'm not afraid to say that I can take a shower anywhere on the planet -- and I even go into the whirlpools and steam baths on occasion, too. I can go to baseball games, drive through tunnels, go over bridges, stay on the 30th floor of hotels, go to the movies, take cruises, meet with dozens of people, and participate in any type of excursion you can imagine. There was a time when I was certain that I would not live to see that day.

I grew up riding dirt bikes and developed into a motorcycle enthusiast, though I waited until I was 43 years old before buying my first real bike -- a 2001 Harley-Davidson Road King. And today, it's another great pleasure. By the way, I'm not afraid to ride my motorcycle anywhere, either.

The Zac Brown Band has a song called *Quiet Your Mind*. It is one of my favorites for many reasons, but its message has been easier said than done. Because just when you think that you've got it all figured out, God has a funny way of bringing it back, as if he's saying, "Hey, buddy, don't get cocky. You're not through with this anxiety thing just yet."

When driving a motorcycle, it's easy to forget that there are situations that are going to make you nervous, and anyone who says that they have driven a motorcycle and never been nervous is lying. It doesn't matter how experienced you are or how long you've been riding, there are still as many idiot drivers and bad traffic out on the road as ever. You have to stay alert and stay careful. But feeling a temporary moment of nervousness isn't the same as experiencing paralyzing fear.

I decided one afternoon I would take my motorcycle out for a ride from my home in southern Rhode Island over to the city of Newport -- one of the most scenic seaside communities anywhere in the country. If you are familiar with Rhode Island's geography, you'll know there is almost no way to get to Newport without travelling over Narragansett Bay via the Newport Bridge, which just happens to be one of the 100 largest suspension bridges in the world.

I remember smiling to myself as I left the driveway that day. I had successfully crossed that bridge on this bike many times -- something I could never have dreamed of accomplishing at one point in my life. The weather that day was spectacular, too -- the sun was shining, the sky was blue, the breeze was refreshing -- and then moments before I reached the foot of the bridge, an all too familiar feeling hit me out of nowhere like a two-by-four in the chest.

What if..?
What if I get to the top and have to stop?
What if I get to the top and want to jump off?
Why the hell am I suddenly feeling this way?

All these thoughts ricocheted around inside my head. I was about to do something I had done successfully many times, and I had even used all my "tools" before I left the house to get myself prepared and "normal." What could be happening?

This incident is what I refer to as "A Bad Thought Day." It happens. When afflicted with this condition for so many years, it's not realistic to expect that it will simply disappear overnight, or even in a month, or in a year. *It is a process.* And even when you do everything right, it will still come back once in a while. It will test you. And it's when you'll need to go back to your trusty toolbox once again. It is a moment like this when you'll need to reflect on what was taught and what you've read, and trust it. I'm living proof that it works, but the process is not like swallowing a miracle pill or receiving an electric shock treatment of some kind. It's all about rethinking, refocusing and realizing what it is and what it can do to you, and then reliving and rethinking that process again.

The first step is to realize that panic and anxiety will not kill you. And I repeat, IT WILL NOT KILL YOU. Despite the extreme levels of panic and anxiety I have lived through, I have never reached level 10. Why? Because in my mind level 10 meant death -- when your mind and body finally give in. When in the midst of an attack of the worst kind, I wouldn't let myself check the VHF radio on my boat because if I suddenly learned the radio didn't work, it would push me to level 10. At 3 a.m., I wouldn't let myself call the hospital from the ski resort because if I learned it was really closed, it would push me to level 10. By not knowing these things, I chose to pretend they were OK, thereby never reaching level 10, and staying alive. The cycle becomes an inescapable internal prison. To be on your way, the first step is accepting that level 10 does not mean death.

When I flew alone for the first time, I did so armed with my toolbox. I would use it to repeat a list of quotes and sayings from movies. Though the quotes come from fiction, they felt real to me and became my magic pill. But remember, there is no magic here. After every panic-filled experience, I could reflect back and realize that no matter how bad it was, I was still alive -- it hadn't killed me. I think back and reflect on those bridges, tunnels, elevators, and sales meetings and ask myself, what really happened there? The situations didn't cause the panic. I did not have the crippling physical feelings first. The feelings were manufactured in my head and caused the anxiety AFTER I had been thinking about them. My mind caused all the physical feelings, too. The bottom line -- I am NOT sick.

Back when I was in my own process of recovery, I would seek out opportunities to "test" myself. One such activity was my trip to Ft. Lauderdale where I would rent a motorcycle and drive it all the way to Key West.

When driving from Key Largo to Key West, you will encounter 42 different bridges over 120 miles including one that is a remarkable seven miles long! The famous Seven Mile Bridge is just as described -- with ocean waters on both sides as far as you can see, and there's nowhere to get off or hide once you're on it. Armed with nothing except my motorcycle and my handwritten list of positive thoughts, I decided I was ready to attempt to cross and conquer the Seven Mile Bridge alone. At this moment, I realized I wasn't testing myself anymore, but living with myself instead.

A shot of the Seven Mile Bridge after I took my ride.

The word "living" is critical here. The first, simplest way to lower your anxiety level from a 9 to a 6 or from a 5 to a 2 is to change your thought process. You need to accept that you will not die from this. You need to accept that you don't need a hospital because although your heart rate might increase; your heart will not explode. In fact, the worst thing that will happen to you is physical exhaustion. Ever since I was a child, I have felt my throat closing, but never to the point where I really couldn't breathe. My head never exploded despite the growing pressure. And in those moments in my life when my agoraphobia was at its absolute worst, in the face of the biggest "what if" of all, I never did pass out.

I rode my motorcycle to the island of Islamorada, which is at the beginning of the Seven Mile Bridge, and stopped. I took a room at a local hotel where I could work on confidence and my anxiety. I was in the middle of the "healing thought process" chapter of my life, but as I mentioned, it does take time. And the longer you have been afflicted, and the stronger it has been, the longer it takes to control it. I had already come a very long way, and given the person I once was, I had achieved much. But being the person that I am, I figured that if I could go up and down an elevator once, and drive to New York alone once, I was healed -- time to move on.

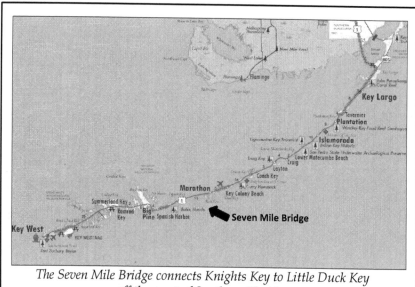

The Seven Mile Bridge connects Knights Key to Little Duck Key off the coast of Southern Florida.

Subconsciously, it takes a long time to stop testing yourself and instead start living with yourself. All the things you wanted to do and dreamed of doing must be achieved through your healing thought process. It's like working too hard or too often after you've experienced an injury; you think you're only going to hurt yourself again. This becomes both an emotional and mental battle. The more you accomplish, the more you want to keep testing... or should I say, living!

I stood on the balcony in this hotel on Islamorada with a six-pack of Corona under my arm and a Kenny Chesney CD playing in the background. I looked out across the awesome, majestic ocean and cried. The tears, however, came from a very different place. This time, I cried because I was happy. In my life, I can count many times that my wife has made me happy, and that my children have made me happy, but this might have been the first time in my life that I had made ME happy. I realized that not only had I made it this far, but that I now knew that I could drive across the Seven Mile Bridge. I could conquer this. And just knowing I could do that meant I could go back home and coach baseball, build a successful business, and lead an enjoyable life outside this prison I had created for myself.

Being an early riser, I woke, ordered breakfast on the beach to watch the sunrise, downed a cup of coffee, and prepared my thoughts for my big ride. But negative thoughts were now seeping in. This was not some quick little ride over a two-mile long bridge like back home -- this bridge was seven miles long. Maybe I wouldn't be able to hold it together that long. I suddenly couldn't eat my breakfast.

Just eight hours earlier I was crying from pure joy and happiness. Now, I was scared to death to go over this bridge. *Son of a bitch!*

What the hell happened? Was it false security? Am I still that pathetic, panic-riddled person?

Fuck it. I decided I would turn around and travel back to Ft. Lauderdale and stay there quietly for a few nights. No one would ever know. I figured I'd just tell everyone that I made it all the way and Key West was beautiful.

Here's where the healing thought process is most important. It's at times like these when you start to question whether you really are getting better -- and you must tell yourself and accept that yes, you are! Just because you have a negative thought, or have a whole day full of negative thoughts, doesn't mean you've failed and need to start all over again. What you need to do is accept and recognize the feelings you are having and know that they are not going to kill you. You are still in control even if you are nervous. It's OK. Let the anxiety come to you and don't fight it.

I pulled out the notes from my toolbox and re-read them, but they didn't seem as inspiring. I got on my motorcycle and started to head north back to Ft. Lauderdale, but for some reason, I turned south and headed for the bridge anyway.

All the way across the bridge, I could feel my anxiety level rise. Level 4. Level 5. Level 6. At the midpoint of the bridge I was already at level 7.

Feeling alive at the end of my ride at the southernmost point in the United States in Key West, Florida.

But a funny thing happened. My anxiety level stopped rising at 7. I was sweating profusely, and my heartbeat was rapid, but I felt I had some control. Suddenly, I felt something new — exhilaration. My heart rate increased a bit more but not from nerves, from joy. Happiness was slowly pushing out the fear.

I got off that bridge at the end and pulled off to the side of the road to take a picture. There were campers, RVs and fishermen everywhere, but I wanted to record that moment. That photo, to this day, hangs on the wall in my office. But I don't use that photo as a source of inspiration; I use it to tell friends the story of my adventure. I don't use it to tell people the story of what I went through, but I use it to tell them the story of where I've been. There is a critical and important difference.

You won't find a degree in psychology or psychiatry hanging on my wall. My lessons were lived, not learned. And I know it works. My words, what I've read, and what I have experienced are all pieces to a puzzle that can help others who suffer from severe levels of panic and anxiety. I promise, it will help.

Since that trip, I have returned to Key West seven or eight times, and four of those times I was alone. And I have driven over that bridge at night, too. Feeling alive through the healing thought process is part of the magic formula. And again, I apologize for using the term magic as there is no magic involved. The healing thought process is not about testing yourself, it's about being alive. It's realizing that the adrenaline rush you get from your fears can be channeled and used differently in profoundly positive ways. Yes, you can fight it, and I fought it for years, crying, and living alone in a self-contained prison, being afraid to move, and just being afraid. Yet now I can enjoy my family and everything God has blessed me with. The key word here is enjoy. I am not going through what I call the Fake False Fear Motion (FFFM) any longer.

The FFFM drained me. But now I am 54 years old, strong, physically fit, and enjoying the best time of my life. And you will, too, as long as you remember that the healing thought process is not about testing. It's all about living.

Just take Zac Brown's advice. "Quiet Your Mind."

15

A PET PEEVE

*We can easily forgive a child who is afraid of the dark,
the real tragedy of life is when men are afraid of the light.*

~ Plato

There is one thing that really pisses me off. It's when someone says, *"Oh yeah, I know what you mean. I get that, too."*

Through the years I've learned to let a lot of negative things roll off my back; it's not productive to carry around anger for no good reason. I've worked my way through so many difficult situations, and during most of those episodes, I didn't understand what I was suffering from. How can I blame someone else for not understanding it if I don't understand it myself?

But the other day I was walking through town and someone from the neighborhood, whom I had not seen in some time, recognized me. He stopped, we exchanged greetings, and we shared a pleasant conversation. For so many years I kept my condition and experiences a closely guarded secret -- so close in fact, my wife and my kids had no idea what I was going through on a daily basis. It's not easy for me to make those details public now. It's something I'm learning to do to help others.

He asked me what I was up to and I decided to step out of my shell. I told him I was writing a book about severe anxiety and panic attacks, to help others who are afflicted. I told him I had struggled with my own agoraphobia and worked for years to overcome it.

"Severe anxiety and panic attacks? Oh yeah, I get those all the time, too... Well, good luck with that!"

Aaarrrgh!

It's very difficult to explain to people in a short conversation what severe anxiety and panic is really like. The way I describe it to someone in a workshop is simple. I ask them to describe it to me so that I am confident they know what severe anxiety really is. Usually they describe a rapidly beating heart, or a dry mouth, or compare it to an out-of-body experience that they get when something scary happens. Not quite. I then ask them to think about the fear they would feel walking alone through an alley at night in a dark, dangerous neighborhood -- completely lost -- with the sounds of angry dogs barking and random screams echoing in the distance. That's the level of anxiety someone with agoraphobia feels *all the time*. But then, someone suddenly jumps out at you from behind a dumpster! You think the worst! That's the feeling of panic someone with agoraphobia experiences during an actual panic attack. The only difference is that a person who jumps out at you is a very real threat, it's rational, where the fear in an agoraphobic's panic attack is entirely created in their mind. In my brain, that terrifying person who jumped out from behind that dumpster is no more than a simple, passing thought.

Again sticking with that analogy, that person or thing that jumped out from behind that dumpster is essentially your bad thought process at work. You are imaging all sorts of bad things that could happen to your body, you think there's something wrong with you, but your mind won't let you leave that dark, terrifying alley. Waiting for the next person to jump out at you is the actual panic attack. People also don't appreciate that these severe attacks can last up to an hour. And it feels much longer than that.

Accepting that these attacks cannot harm you, that they can only exhaust you, is part of the healing thought process even if that process remains terrifying!

To explain the second part of what it's like, I use the analogy of running up ten flights of stairs as fast as you can on a hot, humid summer afternoon wearing a wool suit. And when you arrive at the top out of breath, drenched in sweat, and feeling your heart racing at 200 beats per minute, make believe there is someone else standing there. Now shake their hand and try to carry on a normal conversation. Act as if everything is normal. This is how you feel physically during a panic attack. And this is how I felt when I entered a conference room, stepped into a crowded elevator, or stood to speak in front of a group at a meeting.

Now combine the psychological feelings of the thing jumping out at you from behind the dumpster with the physical effects of running up those stairs.

Now you have it.

Functioning while all this is going on in my system has been an extraordinary experience. Looking back on many of those moments now, I have no idea how I was able to do it. Normal Brian (as I sometimes call myself today) looks back on it now -- and trust me when I say that I don't look back anywhere near as often as I used to -- and wishes I could have felt then the way I do now, and had the tools and healing thought process in place to be able to deal with it better than I did.

If you think you might be a full-fledged agoraphobic, understand that fear and panic is part of normal life. It's when these feelings escalate out of control that they become a condition that needs to be addressed.

Recently, I asked an old friend who has known me since high school to read a draft of the dedication to this book and share his thoughts. About halfway through, he looked up at me over the pages he was holding and laughed out loud. *He truly does not believe that I ever had this affliction. How could he have known?* It's because the fear also made me hide it.

Fear is a powerful emotion. Fear holds many people back. Fear can destroy your life. Everyone experiences fear on some level, but many don't know what *suffering* from fear really is all about. If you have agoraphobia, I know I don't need to explain it any further.

Those who are closest to me, especially my wife and kids, believe me one hundred percent. They understand, but I know they'll never comprehend it fully. Because of the way I was, I faked everything, I lied to everyone, and I hid my fear. And that took away their chance to understand it, too.

I'm neither a psychiatrist nor a psychologist, but I am experienced, and you're holding my Ph.D. in your hands. I ask that you believe and trust me when I say there is a way through it, and that the other side is real. And on that other side, you can be normal again.

So tell me... do you still think you suffer from anxiety and panic attacks, too?

16

THE TEST

The limits I am setting become the prison I am living.

~Anonymous

I was at the point in my life where business was getting better despite myself. I had clients, I had vendors, I had cash flow, but I still had severe anxiety and panic attacks and an undying and growing urge to never leave my house ever again. The success wasn't helping my condition.

It's funny, the more success I experienced, the more that little voice in my head kept saying, "*You're making five to ten times more than what you ever made as a mechanic. Rest. Take a break. Sit on your laurels. You don't have to do this anymore.*"

But then there was that other voice. There is a scene in the movie *Rocky* where Rocky is lying on a bed talking to his young son. His son asks if he ever feels fear when he fights one of those big, monster-like guys.

"Yeah, I do," Rocky answers in that deep throaty Stallone voice. "But then there's that other voice in my head that says I can take the punishment, I can take the fight, I can take the hits, and I can keep going."

Today I am 54 years old and have built a multi-million dollar company, and I'm proud to say there are many people and characters that have provided inspiration to my life. Many people look to teachers for their inspiration, and some people draw it off the wisdom of poets. I tend to draw my inspiration from people I would like to associate with. Although many of these people are technically fictional characters, I know it helps me and inspires me because I can relate to the message. I can relate to characters like Rocky and I enjoy all the Rocky movies (some more than others I suppose, but I don't claim to be a movie critic). I feel inspiration in his words, because as much as I want to rest on my laurels and say that I have accumulated enough money that I can now spend the rest of my life pretending, I can't pretend to be normal and just sweep the anxiety and panic under the carpet. But then another part of me says, "*Screw that. I've come this far with all the drama and I've overcome incredible obstacles along the way; I'll do what I want.*" This brand of panic and fear never sleeps, and yet through it all I was compelled to keep going. I had to -- not just for me, but for the sake of my wife and kids. How could I let them believe the lie I had become? And what would I do later if the business started to falter like my father's did, and if I lost a customer... or two... or three?

I saw what happened to my parents when everything was taken away from them. I lived it right along with them. That particular fear always follows me, and has helped fertilize the roots of my anxiety tree, helping it drill deeper. In the back of my mind, there's nothing there to stop it except my own will and my buddy Danny's voice yelling at me, insisting I keep fighting. In the wreckage that was my dad's company, my fight or flight response kicked into overdrive -- but there was nowhere to go. Nowhere to flee. I had no choice but to fight. And I am glad God granted me that fight or flight choice. I suppose the flight option was there in some form, but it helped me realize how nervous, anxious, scared, and terrified I really was. And I hated that side of me.

As my kids grew up, I used the analogy of a backpack to teach the life lessons I've learned from my own life. I tell them to "put it in your backpack" because you never know when you're going to need it. Feel the fear, and do it anyway... *and keep on doing it.* That's a key. Keep on doing it and the fear will slowly subside, become less and less and become easier to deal with. In essence, keep fighting. And that's what I did.

As I started to become financially successful, one of the first things I splurged on was a small boat. It was a 22-foot Center Console powerboat and I kept it docked in a scenic harbor on the south coast of Rhode Island. I loved the name that was already on the boat, so I kept it -- *Dreamcatcher.* Ironically, I bought it at a discount from someone who was going through a nasty divorce and had placed an ad in the paper. But his bad fortune had become my good fortune, and now it was mine, and it instantly became my fort on the water. And I intended to use it just like that fort I would hide in during my childhood back in Canaan. In fact, back in those days, we even owned an 18-foot aluminum boat powered by a 150 horsepower Mercury outboard motor. We used it to go waterskiing on Twin Lakes. Those were some of the most fun days I can remember, being out on the lake with my dad, my brother, and sometimes my cousins, skiing, fishing, and just having a great time. We'd stay in a cabin owned by a friend of my father's, and it was as safe and as comforting a place as I ever knew. Looking back, I think those good times shaped my affection for the water and how I relate to it as a safe place to be.

Buying the *Dreamcatcher* was a turning point in my life. I was drawn to it, and I viewed it as an opportunity and a tool to help me try and act normal. I figured if I could pretend to be normal, my abnormal feelings would slowly and surely subside. I remember paying for the boat, putting it in the slip, and going over all the details with the seller. It was a Friday, and I was a bit more relaxed than usual, as I knew I was looking ahead to three days of freedom to play with my new "fort on the water" before I had to suck it up and start my anxiety-ridden work week. I pretended I knew a lot more than I did about the craft, and boating in general, and the seller eventually said goodbye and left me standing alone in the cockpit.

Like many states, Rhode Island doesn't require you have a boater's license. So I looked out across the dock past the marina, untied all three lines and started the engine. Slowly but surely I made my way out of the dock and through the guide buoys. I had been on many boats before, so I figured I knew what I *should* be doing. The cove was located in a fairly laid-back neighborhood, populated mostly by local fishermen who were more concerned with their own problems, so no one cared to pay any attention to me. The water was calm so I kept my idle speed low. I steered with one hand and while holding a beer with my other, waved and smiled at other boats passing by me on my left. My anxiety level dropped from three, to two, to one. I felt like I had been doing this my entire life. It was natural. I believed I was meant to be here.

As I passed through the breakwater at the rocky inlet of the marina, I found myself on a body of water known as Block Island Sound. I looked to my left, then to my right, and could see nothing but dark blue ocean clear to the horizon. The water was no longer as calm as it was in the cove, and two to three foot waves now slapped against the side of the vessel, causing it to rock a bit. I then realized I was completely alone.

Anxiety level three. Anxiety level four. Anxiety level five. So why weren't there any other boats around? I had expected to scan the sea and see forty, or maybe fifty other pleasure craft enjoying the morning. I had temporarily forgotten it was Friday and most folks were still at work. I started to seriously worry that I had been too cocky and that I shouldn't have pretended I knew what I was doing, and probably shouldn't have been pretending I was normal in the first place. The "what ifs" were preparing themselves to attack me from all angles. Despite the anxiety that was building in my mind, I pushed forward and headed out into open water.

Dreamcatcher

I could have turned back, but subconsciously, I now know I was testing myself. I was trying to learn how much I could take. I motored along cautiously for about a mile, then looked back and saw an ominous bank of fog about to roll in. I hadn't told anyone I would out here today. Panic kicked in like the start of a speedboat's engine. My anxiety level spiked to nine.

"What if the engine quits?"
"What if I have to swim for shore?"
"What if... oh, dammmit!"

I felt my throat start to close, and my heart began to race a thousand miles per hour. I scrambled around the boat on all fours looking for a bag to hyperventilate into. There wasn't anything. I was angry that I didn't think to bring one along.

I found enough inner strength to slowly turn the boat around and head back to the marina. I could think of nothing except getting past the rocky entrance of the break wall and back into safety. As I entered the cove, I tried to convince myself that the water was too rough out there anyway -- turning back had been the right thing to do. I quickly found my slip and re-tied the boat to the dock. Then I went about washing it down as if I had been out on a three-day cruise, smiling and waving to anyone who might walk by, trying to make it look like I was a savvy veteran boater with decades of experience. I was faking it -- just like I did in my car, on the road, and basically everywhere. But as I stood there portraying the character, I thought about what lie I would tell Robbie when I got home.

"It was a blast! I cruised all the way to Block Island, circled around it, and came all the way back. It was great. I loved every minute of it!"

Did I expect the ocean water to wash away over twenty years of the anxiety and panic I had experienced on land? Did I expect to see hospital signs posted on buoys out there and EMT's floating by standing ready to assist me? I recognized my ego, the fight, and my stupidity all rolled into one moment. The depression was numbing.

And that's another branch of the anxiety tree I haven't discussed very much at all to this point -- depression. Depression can't really be called a true emotion because it wraps itself around so many of the others. It depressed me to know that I had achieved so much in my life yet I still didn't have the one thing I really wanted -- peace of mind.

Not to get off course here (pardon the pun) but there's a song by the band Boston called *Peace of Mind* that sums up my feelings on this and it was a song I would play and sing to myself all the time. Music, akin to movie characters like Rocky, also plays a major role in my motivation.

Now everybody's got advice they just keep on givin'
Doesn't mean too much to me
Lot's of people out to make-believe they're livin'
Can't decide who they should be.

I understand about indecision
But I don't care if I get behind
People livin' in competition
All I want is to have my peace of mind.

Music has always helped me fight off bouts of depression. I never considered myself a true musician, but back in high school, I did play trumpet in the symphonic and jazz bands -- and was pretty good at it, too. I hated reading music, and discovered I could usually pick something up and play it after hearing it only two or three times. But it was the drums I liked more anyway, and to this day, I still have a drum kit set up in my basement where I can make noise. I grab a few beers, head downstairs, and play, making believe there are 10,000 screaming fans dancing in front of me. *Peace of Mind* is a great song, all about a guy trying to live out his life and really doesn't want anything except -- peace of mind.

So why can't I have both? Why can't I have a wonderful family, a successful business and have peace of mind, too? It wasn't like I was doing anything illegal or immoral, I was just trying to live out my life the way everyone else did.

My depression worsened and added to my anxiety. Instead of looking to my boat as an escape of fun and pleasure, I looked to it as a source of depression. Yet another necessary evil that I had to fight to overcome. If the business had not been going strong at that point, I wonder if that would have been the end of me. To endure, I started to view myself like a diabetic -- I had a thing that I just had to live with and get used to because it was going to be this way for the rest of my life. Every boat trip I took sucked. I started to believe that if I was going to ever enjoy something again, I would have to go through at least a level eight panic attack. That was my thing. It's what I was.

My drum kit.

The more I thought about it, the more depression gripped me. But I still went out, played some racquetball from time to time, went to parties with my wife, and through it all, I was fighting. I found myself in the gym more often, too, lifting weights. I would take the family out for breakfast, take our dog to the field and throw the ball around, push my kids on the swing set, then take everyone to the local pool to splash around. I would act like it was a normal, fun day while all the while, deep down, I was focused entirely on "the thing." That anxiety tree was growing and I just could not get rid of it. I would make excuses every chance I got to skip another boat trip. And when the excuses ran out, I'd take the boat out only as far as the breakwater, then quickly bring it safely back to dock.

One afternoon, to take the edge off the anxiety, I downed seven or eight cans of beer before I climbed into the boat. As I headed for the breakwater, I noticed a 40-foot yacht up ahead of me, and I followed him from the southern Rhode Island coast halfway to Block Island -- about 6 miles altogether of open ocean travelling. That's when I decided I couldn't handle it anymore and had better turn back.

As I approached the safety of the marina, my eyes welled up with tears. This was no accomplishment. It was fake. Beer muscles. And I knew I wasn't afraid of the boat or the ocean at all, I was afraid of being alone. A terrible realization. And knowing that depressed me further.

But I was obsessed with fighting it. I went back out a few days later, this time sober. It was early in the morning and my anxiety level was at seven even before I even set foot on the dock. I had been obsessing about the trip all night. The weather was warm, the sun was shining and the wind was dead calm. It was better conditions than anyone could hope to ask for. On the evening before, I bragged to everyone about how great my day on the water was going to be and about how I couldn't wait to get out there. Yet deep down, I was praying that it would rain and give me yet another lame excuse to have to stay home.

So that morning I played the *Theme to Rocky,* shouted at myself in the mirror, and used every self-motivational technique any testosterone-filled maniac would use to get going. My heart was pounding at two hundred beats per minute, yet I kept pushing myself and took the boat deeper and deeper out into the calm, majestic waters of Block Island Sound. I had decided that on this voyage, I would test myself and take myself to the very edge, and accepted that this time, I might not be able to return.

Just like with a ski lift and with an elevator, it's the "what if." I wanted to know. I wanted to feel level 10, even though at that point I didn't yet realize level 10 was unreachable. But I didn't care. I had to find out. I thought about the money I spent on the boat, my employees who relied on me at the office, and most of all my family who loved me. I had to get over this. But more importantly than that, I had to understand this thing.

I took a deep breath and looked down at the ignition key. I was about to cut the engine and create my own level 10. The engine was humming in a soothing rhythm. I thought of Rocky talking to his son. How could I do this? What's the worst that could happen? What if I can't restart the boat? What if the motor just turns over and over and over again?

It was time to find out what level 10 was all about and be alone with my darkest, deepest fear. It was time to be stuck in that tunnel, or on top of that bridge, or in an elevator or to have a full-fledged panic attack in front of those 20 customers in that conference room.

You might be thinking to yourself, "What's the big deal? Just turn the boat off and on and be done with it." But for someone with this level of agoraphobia, being five miles offshore, alone, with no means of assistance is comparable to being stuck alone in a prison cell or trapped behind enemy lines.

My hands still shake as I recount this story even today. It's carved itself into my mind as a permanent memory. I turned that key and the engine went silent. I could hear nothing but the sound of waves gently lapping at the side of the vessel. In the distance, I could see one fishing boat probably twenty miles away and it was unlikely he could see me at all. I remember admiring the fisherman's resolve, and jealous that he could go out anywhere he wanted -- no bad thoughts, no fears, no worries, no "what ifs" -- just go. I remember the smell of the sea, of the oily exhaust from the boat, everything about that day. I did have a radio onboard, but I knew it would take the Coast Guard at least an hour to find me and by then I would have either hyperventilated myself to death or pounded my head into the hull of the boat until I was a bloody, dead mess.

I turned the key and it took eight to ten seconds for the engine to come back to life. I was so happy and relieved I cried. I thought about trying it again, but instantly created a list of 22 excuses why I shouldn't. But it didn't matter. It was done. I had done it. It was time to move on.

For the next two and a half hours, I was normal. I brought the boat back to dock with my head held high and my chest pumped out a little farther than usual. I hopped off and started up random conversations with a couple of guys nearby. We talked and laughed about boating for over an hour. It felt great to be normal.

There's one funny thing I'd like to share here. I find it hilarious that there are people who are terrified to do many of the things I do all the time like selling to new customers, power lifting, or even putting their boat back into the slip. People with my condition never fear the actual acts themselves. I was born to sell, and wonder what I would have accomplished had I not been so panic-stricken. I wonder what competitions I might have won power lifting without this affliction. And believe it or not, just the act of docking a boat poorly in front of other enthusiasts gives some boaters fits. I remember having a conversation and asking why anyone would buy a boat if they were afraid to dock it. Shit, talk about the pot calling the kettle black!

But this boat was my last straw. After this episode, I knew without a shadow of a doubt I was doing this all wrong. I couldn't go through life constantly fighting like this anymore. If I did, I knew I'd never live to see my fortieth birthday. Had I really just bought a $40,000 boat to test my anxiety? Or was I testing my manhood? Or my fear? Am I the only guy to buy a boat just to see how far they could get offshore before they died of a heart attack? Didn't other people buy boats because they wanted peace of mind and relaxation? To be one with the Earth? To be Zen-like? On the drive home, I thought about all these things and cried some more.

But despite the depression, the moment proved to be a turning point in my life. It showed that beyond a shadow of a doubt, I would not die from this – I couldn't. And it also showed me that perhaps something else was going on inside my head that I hadn't yet considered. I had to be smarter. I had to delve further. And I had to continue to test myself until I won it, and if I didn't win it, I pledged to test myself until I did. Maybe that was why God gave me the opportunity to own this boat in the first place.

This story is significant, too, for sending me into another hobby - - reading. I had to find the missing piece and turned to books. I read until I could read anymore. I read while on sales calls, I read in the bathtub, I read on vacation... I just kept reading! Most of the books I read were about anxiety, nervousness or Zen. And the advice they offered worked great until I put the book away and had to go back to face the life I was leading.

In the movie *The Shawshank Redemption*, a prisoner who has spent his entire life behind bars finally receives his freedom. The narrator remarks with one of the most famous quotes in film history, *"He had to get busy livin' or get busy dyin'."* And sadly, the character chooses to take his own life. A few scenes later Morgan Freeman's character is faced with the same decision, yet he approaches the problem differently. He elects to hop a bus and head for the ocean where he intends to live out the rest of his life in peace.

Fight or flight. Fight or flight. It's a shame there isn't more gray area. And that was my biggest mistake. Just because I wasn't able to do it did not mean I couldn't. It meant I was doing it all wrong. It meant I needed to keep testing.

Damn boat...

17

ADVENTURES IN BOTTLE SELLING

Fall down seven times, get up eight.

~ Japanese Proverb

I have a favorite hotel in Carteret, New Jersey. It's the Holiday Inn at Exit 12 right along the New Jersey Turnpike. It's an OK hotel, I guess -- no better or worse than dozens of the other chain hotels that populate the exits along the busy highway. The difference with this hotel is simple: it sits on a hill and has a sign pole that appears to extend hundreds of feet in the air. The sign is so high, in fact, you can see it for miles around. I was able to use that sign to establish a home base for myself whenever I was away from home. As long as I could see that sign, I figured I'd be OK. And that's a very welcome amenity for anyone who has agoraphobia.

I had scheduled an important dinner appointment in Brunswick, New Jersey at Exit 9, which felt like half way around the world to me. The man I was preparing to meet was a major player providing bottles to the automotive industry. And he had invited his son to join us, too, who was poised to soon take over the family business from his father. This account had the potential to be enormous and long-lasting, and I knew I had to make a good impression. But I worried I wouldn't be able to handle it. I hadn't been able to sleep. The anxiety about this meeting had been building in my system for days.

Thank God for the tall Holiday Inn sign
in Carteret, New Jersey.

I thought I had planned that day out perfectly, too. I was aware I needed to burn off the fear and anxiety in some way or I'd never be able to walk through the door of that restaurant, and I was thrilled when I found a full-service gym just ten minutes away. The gym has always served as my sanctuary, and it was where I could really work out my fear and frustration -- I needed to exhaust myself and find my focus before this meeting.

I ran through my usual workout routine. It was mid-July, I was tiring, and the sweat really started to flow. However, I discovered the anxiety wasn't lessening -- it was growing. I then decided to get on a treadmill to run. I ran for over twenty minutes until I couldn't breathe or barely stand up, and found I was completely drenched in sweat. As I ran, all I could think about was this dinner. The pressure. And remember, that's where anxiety does its best work -- in the future. I tried to focus on my favorite Mark Twain quote, "*I've had a lot of worries in my life, most of which never happened.*" But even that wasn't working. I looked at my watch and realized I needed to go. But I also needed to run more. I felt myself starting to go crazy.

I hopped off the treadmill and jogged outside into the late-afternoon July heat to retrieve my suit from the backseat of my car. My hands were shaking so bad with panic I could barely put the key in the car door. I scanned the skyline to see if my Holiday Inn sign would be visible. I knew just seeing it would calm my nerves a little, but I couldn't locate it. It was just too far away. I brought the suit back inside and found myself in one of the ugliest, nastiest men's locker rooms I had ever seen. I doubt it had been cleaned in a year, and the room was populated by a group of scary-looking muscleheads all in various stages of undress, who I had to guess had probably never even seen a suit before. I really should have gone back to the hotel to shower, but time had run out. I tried to think up a great excuse so I could make a call and get myself out of the meeting, but nothing was coming to me.

I turned on the shower and pulled off my workout clothes. Some guy I just trained with and had commented how strong I was walked past me a little too close, and I felt myself spin into a full-fledged level nine panic attack. Then I had a vision: if I didn't get myself under control, I knew I would step naked into the shower, shampoo my hair into a big white lather, then run screaming through the gym, stark-naked, out into the street. Imagine what he and everyone else in this tough Rahway gym would have thought then -- *shit.*

I never did take that shower; instead, I just slipped the suit over my hot, sweaty body. I buttoned up my white shirt now translucent in sweat, knotted-up my tie, buttoned up my jacket, matted down my hair, walked back out to the parking lot and headed for dinner. I was a mess.

I wish I could say it was the first time this had happened. It wasn't. And sadly, it wouldn't be the last.

* * * *

I was only about 24 years-old, and I was embarking on my first real sales call. My father's best sales guy had quit to start his own company, leaving our entire family's business in utter chaos. Since I fancied myself to be my dad's fix-it guy, I decided I had to be the one to go out and try to sell. I didn't feel I had any choice.

So with no training or experience and a box full of bottles, anxiety and fear, I put on my monkey suit and headed across town to visit a well-established company called Bradford Soap.

Bradford Soap was a revered local institution with a 100-year-old reputation as a leader in the personal care industry that made an enormous variety of well-known soaps and related products. I hadn't picked an easy first target. I admit I had no idea what I was doing, but after making probably a dozen cold calls, they figured the only way they could get me off the phone and stop wasting their time was to grant me a meeting. And I already knew from their disinterested tone they wanted nothing to do with me.

I pulled into the company's giant parking lot and turned off the car. I looked up at the massive stone mill building and felt the panic rumble throughout my body. It was only then that I fully appreciated how terrified I was. What the hell was I going to say to this guy? I don't know how to sell anything! Where would I even begin? And perhaps my biggest anxiety was my father; I hadn't told him I was coming here. I was terrified even more of what he might say.

I sat in the waiting room boiling in my own juices until I was called in for the appointment. In my mind, I was expecting to meet with one buyer in an anonymous, quiet office in the back of the building somewhere. As I was escorted in, I realized there was no office -- instead, I was faced with a sea of 200 cubicles where everybody on the floor could hear and see everybody else. It was a dizzying, noisy maze.

The man I was scheduled to meet was on the phone when I got there, so he pointed at the chair in the corner of his cubicle and I sat down. Frantic office activity bustled all around us. The box of plastic bottles I was holding was rattling in my hands as I shook, and I started to worry that with my throat closing so fast, I wasn't going to be able to speak. I could feel my heart beating in my throat.

As I waited, I was beating myself up in my mind. *I can bench press 400 pounds and I'm too chicken to talk to this skinny little guy about bottles for two minutes?* I wanted to play some music and get myself psyched-up, then I would be able to jump up and scream into this guy's face like we'd all do at the gym.

"Hey! You! Buy these bottles from me right now, man! Do it! Do you fucking hear me? We're cheap and right down the road! And you know what? If you don't, I'm going to kick the crap out of you and your supplier, too!"

If I had done that, I don't know if it would have worked or if they would have asked the men in the white coats to come take me away.

When he hung up his phone, I instinctively stood and reached across his computer to shake his hand. Back in those days, computers weren't the skinny Apple and Microsoft desktops and laptops we have today. This guy's computer monitor weighed about 40 pounds and had a hundred wires coming out of the back of it. He also had a four-line telephone on his desk with a spider's web of wires coming out of the back of that, too. As I stood to shake his hand, my left foot got tangled in the wires, and as I sat back down, I sent his massive computer and phone cascading to the floor in an ear-splitting crash of breaking glass and plastic that brought the busy, bustling room to a complete standstill. I can't be sure, but for a split second, my heart may actually have stopped.

The man was cool. He never once flinched or even looked at me. All he did was stand and point.

"Get out of my office."

* * * *

My wife Robbie could see the stress and worry in my face. It concerned her, but she read it as the same, ordinary stress and worry that any young man might face when working around the clock trying to save a struggling business. She had no comprehension as to the profound depth of the panic I carried.

In those days, whenever I found myself in a CVS or other drugstore, I would spend hours carefully looking at all the bottles on the shelves, scanning them for company addresses I could use for a sales call. The problem was that with my family being in this business for so long, we knew all the companies in our area pretty well already. It was rare to stumble across a significant company that we didn't have on file. But on this day, I got lucky. *Autocrat!*

Autocrat is a coffee distributor located in Smithfield, Rhode Island, that was building a business in the extract market, and was producing a coffee syrup that had become insanely popular locally. This was a big account we had not chased before, and they needed a bottle I really wanted to make. I knew we would be the perfect match for them. In fact, it's an account we landed and still service to this day.

When I got home that night, I told Robbie about my lucky find and that I planned to visit them the next morning. She was ecstatic, and possessed a lot more confidence in my selling abilities than I did. Coincidentally, she even happened to know the account since it was a very well-known company in Rhode Island, and she had a feeling that this one was going to work out. She knew how an account like this would mean everything to me, to our company and to our new family. But I looked forward to my trip to Autocrat the next morning with absolute dread. I could feel the anxiety already tingling in my chest. I wouldn't be able to sleep. I feared something terrible would happen. So much was on the line. I was scared to death.

I got in the car that morning and pulled out of my driveway for the 13-mile drive from Cranston to Smithfield. I played the *Theme from Rocky* on my tape deck, then I turned the radio over to something more soothing. After driving a few miles, I pulled over and hyperventilated. I returned to the road and pulled over again a few miles later. I had to find a way to shed this anxiety and irrational fear which at the time I still didn't understand. I thought I was going crazy. It took me three and a half hours to travel those 13 miles.

As I sat in the Autocrat parking lot, my eyes filled with tears and I started to rock and cry like a baby. No matter how hard I tried, I could not go in. I just didn't have it in me. Even with my family and business on the line, on this day, I couldn't do it. I don't remember how long I sat there trying to find the will. But with no other alternative, I re-started the car, turned around and headed for home.

The 20-minute trip back to the house was the longest, most painful drive of my life. The guilt was crushing. I had no idea what I would tell Robbie. I figured I could try to lie again and tell her they didn't want us to make any bottles, but I remembered she already knew the customer. I really didn't know what I would say or how I would say it. I was humiliated, defeated, and was letting her down in the worst possible way.

I pulled up to the house and got out of the car. As I walked to the front door, Robbie bounded out to meet me, her eyes wide and full of anticipation. She looked like a child on her birthday about to receive a really great present. I stood in front of her holding nothing but the bottle I had discovered at CVS the day before.

"So... are you going to make it?" she asked.

"I don't know," I answered.

About fifteen minutes later, I realized she was asking about the bottles.

18

EXPERTS

*I, not events, have the power to make me happy or unhappy today.
I can choose which it shall be. Yesterday is dead, tomorrow hasn't
arrived yet. I have just one day, today, and I'm going to be happy in it.*

~ Groucho Marx

I do not believe that life's challenges are supposed to paralyze you. Instead, I believe they exist to help you learn, grow and discover who you are.

I rarely feel "anxious" anymore, but when those situations do present themselves, I prefer to use the term "uncomfortable" in its place. I hate to use the word anxious. I have accepted that anxiety and panic will never leave me completely, which is why I keep my toolbox near at all times. The tools need to become part of your daily experience and routine as they have done for me.

I have always told my kids that "life doesn't come with an instruction manual." Anyone is qualified to offer advice on any problem and share an opinion. And there are opinions out there at every turn. We live in a very noisy world. It's important to figure out in life who you should listen to and who you can trust.

For me, in business and in life, I have always valued the opinions from those who have been there and done it. I don't want to learn simply about going through the motions, I want to know about the emotional parts, too – I want to hear what it truly feels like to go through all the glorious success and heartbreaking setbacks. Using the analogy of baseball, it's like an all-star slugger who goes through a terrible slump and hires a batting instructor who wasn't even good enough to make it out of the minors. Even if it's great advice, how can that hitter trust it? But if that hitting instructor happens to be a Hall of Fame slugger who is sitting on 30 years of professional baseball experience, the hitter would be foolish to disregard the opportunity to learn from his depth of advice and experiences.

So yes, I believe that living for 40 years with anxiety and panic attacks qualifies me as an expert. To go through what I have experienced and to achieve the success I have qualifies me, at least in my opinion, to mentor others if nothing else.

Recently, baseball superstar Curt Schilling got in trouble for sending a controversial tweet and he was suspended from his baseball analyst job at ESPN. Whether you like or dislike Schilling's political views, there is no doubt he offers a compelling, unique insight into the game of baseball. He has seen it all – American League, National League, playoffs, World Series, awards, championships – delivering his insight from a place of 100% experience. Schilling was replaced by another ESPN analyst, Olympic softball star Jessica Mendoza, an extremely talented broadcaster and athlete in her own right. As I watched and listened to the game that night, I was immediately struck by Mendoza's own depth of insight and analysis. She was great, but for me, it just wasn't the same. Mendoza never took the mound in a World Series game. And even when I agreed with her opinions, or felt I learned something from her insight, it just didn't carry the same weight.

When reading books by experts on agoraphobia and panic attacks, I have the same problem. Many of those books are written by professionals and doctors who have spent their lives studying this condition, but have never actually experienced any of it for themselves. And believe me, I read and read and read and read. I read everything I can get my hands on. But unless the book was written by someone who could express and describe the same feelings I was experiencing, I had trouble identifying and accepting any of the advice they offered.

Today when I speak to groups of people about agoraphobia, I can see them slide forward to the edge of their seat. I can see them hanging on my every word. It's when I know I've reached them. They are suffering, and they now must know exactly how I got from where I was back then to where I am now.

I recently read that there are therapy dogs that have been placed in select airports to help ease the anxiety of people who are afraid to fly. This got me thinking that I needed to explain the difference between a common fear or phobia and agoraphobia. I find that I am still uncomfortable when flying and still uncomfortable when I have to speak in front of a group. But notice I used the word "uncomfortable" and not the word "afraid." When you have a fear of spiders or fear of lightning, these are fears or phobias you can both pinpoint and work on. It's when you are afraid to leave your own house and afraid of everything outside it that you reach a point that is debilitating. It is not one particular phobia. It is an irrational fear of all places outside your safe place. It can't be pinpointed in the same way. And that sucks.

Life may not come with an instruction manual, but I wanted this book to become as close to one for overcoming agoraphobia as possible. If it helps, picture me sitting across from you, face-to-face, looking back into your eyes. As we connect, I will share the feelings I have experienced through my own healing thought process. As you listen to my advice, understand it comes from a lifetime of positive and negative moments. Real experience. There is no need to go it alone via trial and error as I did. Let's do this together.

19

THE TOOLBOX:
THE HEALING THOUGHT PROCESS

You gain strength, courage, and confidence by every experience in which you really stop to look fear in the face. You are able to say to yourself, "I have lived through this horror. I can take the next thing that comes along." You must do the thing you think you cannot do.

~ Eleanor Roosevelt

As a mechanic working in my father's blow molding shop, I became familiar with and learned to respect many different tools and what they could do. They were my lifeline. If a machine was down, it meant we were losing money, and it had to be repaired and returned to operation as fast as possible. Having access to the right tool in my toolkit and knowing how to use it could save minutes, hours, and even days of headaches and risks to the health of the company -- a constant source of intense anxiety.

Throughout this book, I have made mention of using tools from my toolbox to treat my own anxiety and panic attacks. The tools I use are quite similar to the tools I might use to repair a poorly operating machine. In any given crisis, I need to know what tools I have available and I need to know how to use them to fix the problem. And knowing that a problem could arise at any time, I had to be vigilant and ready.

In the middle of difficulty lies opportunity.
~ Albert Einstein

Learn to Drop Your Armor

In theory, armor exists to protect you -- it's something to wear and hide behind when an enemy attacks. The first truth you must realize and accept is that the whole healing and thought process surrounding anxiety and panic attacks <u>will not kill you</u>. Therefore, raising your armor to fight "the thing" is not the answer, and the sense of security your armor provides is a false one. Remember... what good can armor do when fighting yourself? Put down your shield and your sword and allow the fear to come to you. <u>Feel the fear!</u> It took me 35 years to realize that this fear, no matter how terrible and intense it might become, was not able to kill me. I tested myself over and over again believing that it could become worse and lead to my eventual death. But no matter how close I came to level 10, I would never quite reach it. I could not die from it. Once you accept that these attacks are survivable, you are well on your way to recovery.

Say the Words " Nobody's Coming"

I wish I could remember where I first read the words "nobody's coming" because these two simple words are not only very true but have been life-changing. When I was alone on my boat, in the shower, or in an elevator, why would I always wish someone else would be there with me? Why did I want them sitting in the car with me, or standing near me in the elevator? The reason was simple. If something happened, which of course it never did, there would be someone there ready and available to call for help. I would always imagine the very worst – passing out, choking to death, a heart attack, breathing difficulty, going crazy... even killing myself. It took me years to come to the realization that I had never actually been in a situation bad enough where I needed the other person to make that call. You will learn and eventually come to appreciate that you have both the will and the power to let that fear come to you, let it pass through you, and let it leave you. You do not need anyone else. Nobody's coming – and that's a wonderful thing – because the healing thought process doesn't start with them, <u>it starts with you.</u>

Patience is the key to contentment.

~ Mohammed

Visualize Good, Not Bad

I'm not the first person to advocate positive visualization, and I've come to appreciate that the reason it's so popular is because it really does work. Every time I was alone I would think about and visualize all the bad things that were about to happen to me. Why? Why on God's green earth would someone *want* to think about bad things happening to them? But for some reason, that's precisely what I did, and it took a long time for me to realize that I was bringing these thoughts on myself. It might sound a tad corny, but just telling yourself (out loud if you need to) that "it's time to heal" can matter. Simply close your eyes and picture yourself placing a small bandage over the bad thought. There is another simple trick that worked well for me, too. I would wrap a rubber band around my wrist, and each time I realized I was having a bad thought, I would snap the rubber band hard enough to inflict a little pain, but not so hard as to break the skin. (You might need a big box of these rubber bands that first week!) You'll be amazed at the number of bad thoughts you experience in a day. What constitutes a bad thought? Usually, they come in the form of a question intended to enhance your insecurity: "What if?" "How long will this take?" "Will I be alone?" "How many people will be there?" "How can I get out of this?"

Now admittedly, these are the easy ones. When you really stop to think about it, and again I know this from years of experience, it is possible to have twenty, thirty, forty, even fifty of these bad thoughts in a single minute! With so many negative thoughts flying around in your mind, it becomes easy to see why you believe you can scare yourself to death. It's like getting yourself caught up in a swarm of those little black flies they call "no-see-ums." The first couple of bites irritate you, but after about fifty of them, the bites feel like they are coming from horseflies, you feel like you can't take it anymore, you think you will be devoured alive, and you want to scream. Another technique is to keep a written record of all your bad thoughts for a day, breaking them down into hours and minutes. This will help you see how these thoughts have fed the roots of your anxiety tree and helped it grow. The total number of these thoughts will astound you. And it's almost incomprehensible to think about and total the number of bad thoughts you've had in your lifetime. (I'm sure you'd never let anyone talk to you the way you talk to yourself!) Changing your thought process in this way is extremely hard to do, and it won't happen quickly. But you're taking advice from an expert here. I'm someone who has been through this and come out the other side. You can and will, too. Let it come. You don't need anyone to help you.

Act the part, walk and talk exactly as if
you are already the person you want to be.

~ Brian Tracy

Act As If

The human mind is extremely powerful. While experiencing the panic I've talked about in this book, it was very difficult for me to act normal. Why? Because in my mind, I was convinced I wasn't. And though there wasn't anything physically wrong with me, the mental stress caused many illnesses and physical manifestations to develop. Once you realize the substantial power your mind has over you, your actions and your beliefs, you can then move ahead and -- "act as if."

First you must visualize doing the right thing, then second, you must know it's the right thing to do, but that's still not enough. You must still actually do it.

I see myself stepping into that elevator and can see the door close. I know it is irrational to be afraid, and that this elevator trip is a good thing for me to do. I will now act as if there is no fear and step into the elevator.

If your agoraphobia is bad, then "act as if" it's not. I don't claim this step is easy, it isn't. But it's important and where the title of this book originates -- *I'm scared to death and I will do it anyway.*

When you stop and think about it, being scared to death is easy. The hard part is acting when you are scared. How much can you accomplish "acting as if"? Put humbly, when I think about all the bad moments I endured on all those sales trips over 30 years, yet I was still able to build a multi-million dollar business, I find it almost surreal. All the while, I did it acting as if I was normal. I still experience fear like everyone else of course, but it's a normal brand of fear like fear of the unknown, fear for your kids' safety, or fear of your own health. These fears are in no way debilitating. When you can walk, and act, you become the person you've always wanted to be. It's at that moment that you'll realize you've made it – physically, mentally, professionally, financially and most important – emotionally. It's OK to not fear everything every minute of every day. Act as if you want to do it. Act like who you want to become. Your mind has truly amazing power. Just act as if...

The Longer, The Longer

Patience. The longer you have suffered from anxiety and panic attacks, the longer it will take you to go through this healing thought process. It's as simple as that. There is no magic pill you can swallow, and you must do everything you can to avoid becoming hooked on Valium or Xanax or any one of many physically addictive drugs your doctor might prescribe. These drugs tend to only ghost your fears, not eliminate them. Under the influence of these drugs, the roots of your anxiety tree continue to grow, not disappear. Think about how long you've been affected by your own anxiety and fear and think about how intense those moments had become. Give yourself permission to take your time with the healing thought process. Remember, getting mad at yourself is a negative thought -- snap that elastic band! Act as if. Be happy. Be patient and the negative thoughts will subside.

> *To achieve calm, we require patience.*
>
> ~ Anonymous

Bad Words

In a previous chapter, I talked about the things I would do to "test myself." This two-word phrase is an example of bad words you need to avoid. There is no such thing as testing myself -- it's really called living my life. I accept that there will be times in my life when I will feel fear, but now I use the word "uncomfortable" in its place. In fact, take the word "fear" right out of your vocabulary, too. If you say the word "fear," snap that rubber band! If you say the phrase, "test yourself," snap that rubber band again! We live in a world that can be mean and nasty at times, and you need to know these words and phrases are merely skin deep and you cannot allow them to penetrate your soul. Being angry or upset are very real and important emotions; I've learned that. But if the anger and emotion originate with those bad words, snap that rubber band again! This change won't happen overnight, but over time, you will get better.

Avoid Caffeine

Caffeine is a stimulant that has a direct effect on the nervous system. That's a fact. When I was working my way through the healing thought process, I totally eliminated caffeine from my life. All the books I have ever read on this topic might disagree on which vitamins to take or which diet to follow, but they all warn of consuming caffeine. I've always enjoyed a lot of coffee. During my testing period, I didn't realize the profound effect it was having. But it wasn't just an addiction to caffeine that fertilized my anxiety tree, it was an addiction to the coffee shops and coffee breaks, too. If I was getting ready to work out, in the factory repairing a machine, or anywhere else, coffee offered a bit of an escape. And there I was with one foot on the gas and one on the brake. My mind was trying to fix the problem by relaxing but pouring fuel into my adrenal glands to produce more cortisol. To this day I avoid all stimulants (including chocolate) before I fly or before I give any big presentation. Don't feed the anxiety tree!

Stop Drinking

Ask everyone who knows me, and I guarantee they'll all say the same thing -- Brian loves his beer! And boy, do I! Someone once joked that I wouldn't buy a boat if I didn't like beer.

Preparing for my wedding day
with lots of beer, 1986.

Drinking to me is a celebration, but it wasn't always like that. I once drank with the sole intention of masking all my fears and anxieties. It was how I tried to cope. And now it is just the opposite. In fact, when I'm in a bad mood, or when something goes wrong in my business or in my family life, I don't feel like drinking at all.

I have explained that I would drink to hide my fears in many places and in many situations, and I did this for several years. Although carrying a buzz around in my head helped me temporarily forget, it didn't fix anything. In fact, it made it significantly worse. Once the buzz wore off, the rubber-band effect of sobriety would spike the fear and anxiety to higher levels than before even quicker. You need to learn to smile and not let booze mask your anxiety. Unfortunately, alcohol has become an essential crutch for many agoraphobics, so there will likely be setbacks when avoiding drinking. But do your best. Every time you turn to the bottle to take the edge off that anxiety and fear, you will be setting back your own progress by months. Your desire to get better needs to be stronger than your desire to have temporary fun. For many, this means never drinking another drop of alcohol ever again. But for others, like me, if you make the decision to continue to drink socially, then you need to re-learn how to do it. It sounds strange, but it's true. Alcohol is your enemy when you are experiencing anxiety. Learn only to drink when you are happy, not sad. It's an obvious point but an important one: you can't hope to work through problems when you are drunk.

True courage is cool and calm. The bravest of men have the least of a brutal, bullying insolence and in the very time of danger, are found the most serene and free.

~ Lord Shaftesbury

Good Days, Bad Days

As I worked my way through the healing thought process, there were times I figured I was going nuts and was destined to end up in an insane asylum somewhere. There were many times, such as that trip over the Seven Mile Bridge, where I felt great, then suddenly experienced the fear out of nowhere, and believed that I'd fail and would need to start all over again. There was another time I recall feeling relaxed, walking into my son's and daughter's school to meet with teachers. Then suddenly, I found myself stuck in a classroom behind a closed door with a dozen strangers where my heart started to race and the stress started to build.

There were many times I assumed I was healed, that it was all over, and then cruelly when I least expected it, it would return and I'd be set back. I learned that this is something that's just going to happen. It must be accepted. It is part of the process. You might feel great for as long as six months or more, only to have that damned anxiety tree rear its ugly tentacles out of nowhere. It's demoralizing, but it's not failure.

And that's when you use the next tool -- this book! It's when you say that hey, this is expected. I'm not alone. This guy Brian has been through it. I will do it, too. Just because you experienced a bad moment does not mean that tree is growing, it's only reminding you that it's not completely dead. Act as if, snap that rubber band, take notes, and let your mind go to another place. Concentrate on getting yourself off that bad thought merry go-round. Accept that it's part of the process.

At 54 years old, even with full knowledge of this process and how it works, I still have bad thought days. I no longer have to worry about selling to new customers, having dinner in restaurants, going to movies, or travelling. But I still become uncomfortable flying or speaking in front of large groups. One of the ways I get through it is by telling people about it. I learned that despite the number of people out there who don't fear flying, there are many that do. Feeling that you are not alone can help.

You might remember the TV weatherman Willard Scott from NBC's "The Today Show." He had a terrible fear of public speaking. Each day, just before his weather segment was set to air, he would have a brief conversation with the show's host, Bryant Gumbel. The back-and-forth banter was planned, and was designed to help take some of the focus off Willard before his segment. The interaction would drop his anxiety level from 6, to 5, to 4, to 3... and help prepare him to deliver his report. This happened every single morning, and it was his willingness to admit his anxiety to Bryant and his colleagues that helped him overcome it. Sometimes admitting the problem helps make people feel like they are normal. Don't beat yourself up if you are experiencing a bad day, just act as if, let it go, and move ahead.

I want to reiterate one more time that the healing thought process can take a very long time to complete and have its desired effect. You need to give yourself credit for every small achievement -- a good solid pat on the back -- even for reading this book. It shows you want to get better. Turning that corner is not easy, and I admire you for simply trying it.

I've been there and understand the physical and emotional wars of agoraphobia, but that doesn't mean I would ever discredit the advice of any psychiatrist or psychologist; in fact, I encourage and welcome it because it is needed. (I wish there had been good advice available to me all those years ago or, more importantly, had sought it out so I would <u>know</u> what it was.) The lessons I've learned and what I've been through is a path, I believe, that was chosen specifically for me. I was raised Catholic, and I do believe in God. Like many Catholics, I never miss church on the big holidays like Christmas, Good Friday and Easter, but I admit I only sprinkle in another 10 to 15 Sunday visits throughout the year. I consider myself a very spiritual person and believe that we all need help from someone, or from somewhere, at certain times in our lives. I feel spiritual when I'm alone on my boat, gliding along the ocean waves. I feel spiritual when I'm on the beach listening to the waves lap up onto the beach. You might find that same inner peace and

THE ANXIETY TREE

tranquility elsewhere in your own world. These just happen to be my special places.

My hope and dream is that after you read my book, you will continue to use it as a template and guide to motivate yourself through your own healing thought process to get better. "Scared to death... do it anyway" is not a demand, it's my way of wishing you well and saying -- trust me. There is a way to get there.

May you live the life you imagined.

20

THE PHYSICAL TOOLBOX:
INTENSE FOCUS TRAINING

*You never know how strong you are
until being strong is the only choice you have.*

~ Cayla Mills

The second part of the toolbox and healing thought process is not mental. It's physical.

A key physical element of anxiety is adrenaline -- a hormone (also known as epinephrine) that is produced by your adrenal glands and is released into your bloodstream when you find yourself in a frightening situation. Adrenaline assists the body with the increase of blood flow to muscles, the output of the heart, and increases your blood sugar, among many other things. It is the centerpiece of the "flight or fight response" inherent in all of us. We rely on adrenaline to quickly escape a burning building in the middle of the night, fight off an attacker, or run from a wild animal. In agoraphobics, the subconscious mind can open up that adrenal gland at any time whether it's needed to react to real danger or not. By the way, living in constant fight or flight mode is exhausting.

When I was flying, I wanted to do as many physically distracting things as I could to reduce that impending release of adrenaline. I thought about asking if they'd let me do push-ups in the aisles, and thought about squeezing myself into those little toilets to do sit-ups, too. But this obviously wasn't practical. I would be forced to spend my time sitting still, challenging myself with small pieces of paper, keeping my mind busy, and avoiding the pitfalls of the dreaded "what ifs."

Through weightlifting, I created what I called Intense Focus Training (IFT) which helped engage and direct the adrenaline and cortisol in my system. This training is similar to putting blinders on a horse -- it allows you to focus your training on one particular activity, one particular set, one particular rep, and one particular moment in time while blocking out all the distracting stimuli around you. My physical training philosophy hasn't changed since my early twenties, except that now my thought process allows me to use this tool to alleviate anxiety becoming physically stronger and mentally tougher together. Utilizing this IFT training, I can focus all my energy on one lift, or one moment, at a time.

To be honest, I can't take complete credit for this approach as many bodybuilders and weightlifters through the years have successfully implemented elements of this training technique, including Arnold Schwarzenegger, Franco Colombo, Mike Katz, and Mike Mentzer among many others. However, the weightlifter who most closely matches my own workout philosophy is six-time Mr. Olympia bodybuilding champion Dorian Yates.

Yates was able to summarize my own thinking with one simple analogy -- hammering a nail into a piece of wood. Essentially, he sees training as driving that nail. Once it is all the way into the wood, if you keep hitting it, you only damage the wood. The nail can move no further, therefore once you've finished, move on. Stop hitting that nail. When I first read this analogy I thought, "Holy shit! That's what I've been doing mentally, in my own head!" I realized that I had been using this technique for over 15 years to focus on any single issue -- a new customer, a meeting, any specific fear, or anything I wanted to succeed at doing, except I wasn't stopping, I was still hitting that nail over and over again. I would visualize what I wanted to accomplish except I would over train myself into absolute, positive failure.

The goals I envisioned, whether it was adding more weight or taking another rep on a particular exercise, had been met. Reaching these goals gave me the confidence I needed to use my adrenaline <u>when</u> and <u>where</u> I was supposed to. This is where I needed my fight response to be. To this day, I still get that very same feeling when I enter my gym. These days I lift alone in my own gym, but I still continue to try and compete with my own personal bests and break physical barriers. Breaking these barriers has enabled my mind to understand the difference between when adrenalin, anxiety, and control is necessary -- <u>and when it is NOT!</u> This example of IFT training, in addition to my healing thought process, has helped me focus on one goal at a time, reach it, and move on to the next. I continue to use small blocks of wood as well as a nail for this goal setting to this day.

When you weight train, your goal is to overload your muscles so they replenish themselves and grow. Yates' philosophy has helped me because by the end of my workout, I realized this overtraining would cause anxiety, not alleviate it. I thought by doing more I would release more adrenaline. It was quite the contrary. I realized the nail was in the wood. I needed to stop before I damaged the wood any further.

Over the course of my anxiety and panic-filled life, I never truly understood how and why I was driven to weight training other than to get bigger, stronger, more confident, and walk around with an ego. As I got older I got smarter, and came to realize I was intentionally exhausting my adrenal glands, but in a good way. Essentially I was giving those overactive glands something to do.

Just a sampling from the wood block and nail collection in my "Motivate for Success" office.

By focusing on one fear that I had and using weight training, and exerting all my strength and attention and adrenaline I had into that one lift, I was able to overcome many obstacles. I have always said that if I was able to lift weights when first meeting a new customer, the adrenaline would be dissipated and I would be... well... the normal Brian! Instead, I would go into meetings and sales calls exploding with anxiety. And there was certainly no way I could stop and bench press for a while in the hallway, in the elevator, or on the tarmac of an airport. I always thought how great it would be to be able to do that.

Initially, my personal powerlifting training regimen started out like everyone else's with the basic goal of just trying just to build muscle and get bigger. However, there is another critically important part of this process that I discovered that needs to be explained.

When I first started to train, like most people, I would train along to whatever music was playing in the gym at the time. Songs from my favorite bands like Boston, Kansas and similar acts really got me going, and in fact, seemed to get everyone in the gym going, helping us all spur on big rushes of adrenaline, cortisol and energy. The inspiration for IFT came from this effect. And later in life, whenever I would go out to see a client or board a plane, and after I started to "heal" through the healing thought process, the importance of this physicality (this so-called physical response) became more evident to me. I learned to use my time in the gym to focus on the release of adrenaline to fight against the weight I was lifting. I use the word "fight" here cautiously, however -- it is the only time that people with anxiety problems should use the "fight or flight" response of their adrenal glands to fight when they are not in the process of defending themselves.

I found that by focusing my workouts in this way, my intensity level in the gym became incredible and it helped me move more weight than ever before. As I started to develop my healing thought process, I used IFT to push myself in the gym and get rid of the leftover adrenaline. By focusing on the music, competing ONLY with myself, keeping a detailed diary of the weight I had lifted (to this day I have book where I recorded every single rep I have done since lifting as a teenager), and pushing myself harder and harder to break even the smallest of personal records, I found myself both exhausted and exhilarated by the time I was done with each workout.

But I learned something else. On days I was outside the gym and I heard music playing from Boston, Kansas, Styx, or one of the other bands I enjoyed while working out, I would feel that same rush of adrenaline. It was an effect I compare to Pavlov's famous experiment with his dogs. I also discovered the same thing would happen when I watched one of the "Rocky" movies during a flight. Essentially, I was turning a positive situation into a negative one.

It's important to remember that the way you train and the thought process you use to train is not just about getting in shape – that's a byproduct of the IFT training method. My technique focuses on how to release that adrenaline by pushing yourself harder and faster in a short period of time, a training technique that as it has turned out, I have been doing for over 30 years without even knowing it. I think I started to realize what was happening in my late 20s and early 30s when I was participating in powerlifting competitions and a very nice calm would come over me after my lifts. I found out later it was the release of endorphins. But I also learned that if I focused on my situational anxieties, every time I trained I could push those fears away. Now I can actually feel the burning of the adrenaline as I lift. But of course it took years for this to become a common occurrence.

My IFT gym within my Motivate for Success facility.

People have always commented on my dedication to training. Whether I am on vacation, whether I stay out late, or whether I travel for business, I will never miss a workout. I will get up at 4 o'clock in the morning if I need to, or I will train at 12 o'clock at night; it is now part of my personal make-up. My wife used to laugh at me when I would drive home from New York and then immediately go down in the basement and run on the treadmill. I did this to release the built-up adrenaline and it would help me sleep like a baby. When you realize the effect your mind can have on over body, and how this IFT training method works, you will not want to miss a workout no matter where you might be. Training heavy, training hard, and training with intensity happens to be my way of releasing adrenaline – and I understand it doesn't have to be yours. I have successfully incorporated this type of training using simple push-ups, sit-ups, isometrics or nothing more than your own bodyweight. There is always a way.

So now I use my mind to differentiate those moments I feel anxiety coming on. It might be on a chairlift, in an airplane, on a sales call, crossing a bridge or in any other place that brings on that usual sense of fear, or NOW in these cases, exhilaration! This was the very thing I talked about when I drove over the Seven Mile Bridge in Key West. It was not fear, it was exhilaration, and was part of the IFT process that was helping me get to the other side. It has become the most important tool in my toolbox. The IFT training was helping me realize that pushing in this way with everything was undoubtedly helping me deal with many scary situations... and here's why. The spike in the adrenaline in my system was so high while I was lifting and working out, it matched the adrenaline I was feeling emotionally while crossing that bridge. After years and years of suffering, I realized that level 10 wasn't death -- death wasn't coming -- but level 10 could also mean complete exhilaration, happiness, the exact opposite of fear.

I still train using intense focus methods, and for those people who don't lift weights, it is just as easy to get the adrenaline and other hormones rushing through your system by using nothing more than push-ups, sit-ups and your own body weight. I am not a personal trainer, but I have many years of experience training and my philosophies have been proven by others who are. Muscle tension, isometrics, weightlifting, bodybuilding... whatever you call it, it's all you against you. And essentially it's the adrenaline that's pushing you to walk, jog, run, or exercise and push you one more rep, or one more mile.

Some people claim that simple exercise can help ease anxiety and panic, and they are not totally wrong. But it's helpful to understand the reasons behind it. I believe using exercise and incorporating these IFT principles is far more productive and effective than blindly working out. Remember that anxiety starts mentally then evolves into physical reaction. If you utilize smart physical activities along with these IFT principles and place your complete focus on any fear, small or large while training, it will work to ease your anxiety. I'm living proof. You will be teaching your adrenal glands how to work the correct way and give you control, helping you go over that bridge, through that tunnel or run that extra mile.

Get on a treadmill, do some push-ups, or go to the gym. What you do isn't that important. But use that time to not only become more physically fit and healthy, but use it to also overcome and control your panic. I am stronger and healthier today at 54 years old than I've been at any time in my life. And I'm panic free. This power has changed my life.

21

IT NEVER REALLY GOES AWAY

The whole secret to existence is to have no fear.
Never fear what will become of you, depend on no one.
Only the moment you reject all help are you freed.

~ Buddha

It's hard to call any one chapter in this book the most important because anyone who suffers from anxiety and panic experiences the process a little differently. Any of the chapters in this book might be the trigger -- the lynchpin, the connection, the rocket -- that launches the reader on their own path to recovery and a better life.

But despite this, I still think this chapter is the most important. Because no matter how successful you become at managing and overcoming agoraphobia, there is one sad truth that you will not be able to escape. It never really goes away.

I am reminded of a song by Nickleback, "Feelin' Way Too Damn Good." I play the drums as a hobby and I've listened to thousands of songs. Most of the time, the lyrics escape me as I focus on the drummer working out the beat in the background. But sometimes the lyrics stick and offer me real meaning.

> *I feel like I'm constantly dreaming.*
> *'Cause something's gotta go wrong.*
> *'Cause I'm feeling way too damn good.*

We have a summer home on Cape Cod and are able to spend a good deal of time there as a family. Of all the places I've been fortunate enough to visit, I think the Cape has to be my favorite. There is something about driving over the Sagamore Bridge and merging onto the Mid-Cape Highway that speaks to me of escaping to paradise. It's hard for me to convey the feelings of peace and contentment that I experience.

Several months ago, something strange happened. We had decided to go to the Cape for a long weekend as a family. So as I always do, I set out on Thursday afternoon alone to get the house ready -- turn on the air-conditioning system, uncover the yard furniture and stock up the fridge with beer. And that motorcycle ride from my house to the Cape in the middle of a perfect New England summer day is one of the most enjoyable parts of the weekend.

As I rode, I felt at ease, smiling with anticipation. Up ahead, I could see traffic thickening and the steel buttresses of the Sagamore Bridge appearing overhead right on schedule. Suddenly I started to feel unexpectedly anxious. Was it the summer heat? The traffic? I couldn't be sure, but I could feel my anxiety level starting to climb. I started to focus on my fear of bridges, and I swear, I hadn't been remotely bothered by a trip over this bridge in over ten years. Then I realized that when I got to the house, I would be all alone. My anxiety level was rising from three... to four... to five.

I became angry at myself. I was really pissed, too! I stopped at a red light and pounded the handles of the bike with my fists. I had started to fight it just like I did when I was in my twenties. Old habits are hard to break.

What the fuck, Brian, I thought we were done with this?

I gripped the motorcycle handles tighter and as I approached the bridge I could feel my body physically shaking. My fight or flight response was in full operational mode. I could sense my heart pumping a steady flow of cortisol through my veins.

In the old days, I would have stopped. I might have turned around and headed home, telling the family that I was sick, or that the motorcycle was broken, or creating some other ridiculous lie. But on this day, I was equipped with the tools I needed to repair this breakdown. I began to focus on a favorite quote, "truth is always the companion of calm."

Another saying I like to meditate on is from Lucinda Bassett, founder of the Midwest Center on Stress and Anxiety, who said, "don't let a bad day scare you." Yes, even after all these years, all these attacks, all these lies, and all this self-realization, I still have to pull out my toolbox on a bad day. I've learned to have that toolbox ready at all times, wherever I go, as I never know when the "The Thing" will elect to once again rear its ugly head. I have learned to harness the power of my subconscious mind, which is far more powerful than you think, to engage my healing thought process.

In less than three minutes, my anxiety level dropped from five... to four... to three... to two. I began to realize I was the victim, again, of my own bad thoughts. There had been some problems the day before at work, and I had stayed up far too late the night before at a party, so I was working on two to three hours of sleep at best and had been pounding the caffeine that morning. Just like a virus that attacks when you're tired and your immune system is down, bad thoughts do the same. No matter how cured you think you are, those bad thoughts are out there lurking, waiting for you to let down your guard.

So I turned that bad thought process into a good thought process. I said to myself, "this is only anxiety. I won't die from this. I've been over this bridge a hundred times..." I prepared to "act as if." I thought about the fun we would have that weekend. I smiled.

As the anxiety started to escape my body, I experienced a tingling feeling all over. The more I smiled, the better I felt. My fingers loosened their grip on the handlebars, and I said aloud, "it was only anxiety." I was relieved that everything in my toolbox was there to help me.

The biggest step is recognizing that it's only anxiety, nothing more. Years ago, I would have followed that realization with, "Yeah, but..." And now today, the thought doesn't cross my mind because I know the tools are there, and like that old screwdriver you might not need for years, my confidence rises just knowing I can rattle around in there and pull it out whenever I need it.

The whole experience only lasted three or four minutes; in the old days, it might have lasted hours. As I moved ahead to finish the remaining twenty-four miles of my journey on the Mid-Cape to the house, traffic eased and the temperature dipped to a perfect 78 degrees. In just two miles, I was happy and normal again.

Anxiety and panic will never go away for me completely. I will experience it the rest of my life. And that's OK.

Acceptance -- it is the final and probably most important means that keep all the other tools within the healing thought process together, safe inside, and ready to use.

Many members of my family, as well as several good friends, were expected to be visiting that weekend. But before that happened, I had some time to myself to hit the beach, read a good book and relax.

And no matter what happens that weekend, or what may occur in the rest of my life, my dependable toolbox will be right there with me wherever I go.

22

FINAL THOUGHTS

"No one saves us but ourselves. No one can and no one may.
We ourselves must walk the path."

~ Buddha

I spend a lot of time alone these days. Some people might think that makes me a loner, but it's far from the truth. Years ago if you caught me alone, it would have been a real oddity; I needed to have others around to maintain my sanity.

Where I am in my life now, I have learned to enjoy being alone with my thoughts. It's not like it used to be. And these are normal thoughts, by the way, they're not thoughts of despair, anguish, depression or those dreaded "what ifs."

One of the reasons I like being by myself is that it allows me to relive those parts of my life that once terrified me. There is a Kenny Chesney song with the line, "the sun's going to shine someday, I hope." Well for me, that sun is shining, and it started the day I learned how to deal with panic and anxiety, and since that day, that sun gets a little brighter and a little bit warmer.

It is now 11:30 at night as I circle a buoy at Conanicut Point near the Beavertail Light here in the waters of Narragansett Bay. It is so dark I can barely see my hand in front of my face, and the ocean air is heavy, humid and warm. I reach down and switch off the engine of my boat – but this is not a test. The testing is over! This is a moment of joy.

It happens to be one of those weekends where my wife is off visiting with her mother, and my kids are off somewhere else busy building their own lives. So there is no guilt having all this fun without them! I peer through the darkness to the south across the Atlantic, the boat is gently bobbing up and down and suddenly I see the dim lights of another boat – perhaps a tanker -- many miles away. I am sitting at the stern, caught up in a very spiritual moment, thinking about how lucky I am, how far I've come, and how exciting and rich my life truly is.

Feelings of bliss often come into our lives in spurts, and this is one of those times. Many people feel happy but have that happiness eventually tugged away by concerns about something in the future. That's called normal worry – and that's life. But it's not for me. Not tonight, at least.

Right now I'm six miles off the coast with a heart full of joy and nothing but good thoughts on my mind. I have about 16 miles to go to port. I plan to bring the boat in slow, starting near Newport and travelling at about 10 knots, I will travel under the vast Jamestown-Verrazano Bridge, cruise through the bay, and enter the friendly waters of Wickford Harbor. Once in the harbor, I'll dock, turn the volume on my Kenny Chesney CD down low, then rinse the boat down. I will text my wife to wish her a good night and tell her that I love her and then hop into bed at about 1:00 a.m. Small riffs of waves will rhythmically slap against the side of the boat and I know I'll be fast asleep in under fifteen minutes.

For years, people have said, "*man... I wish I was you*" and I fought them. "*Oh, yeah, jerk? Do you have any idea what I went through?*" In truth, I have always wished I could have had that life they all thought I was having, too. For much of my life, I didn't want to be me. But tonight, at this very moment, at this very point in my life, right where I am, I can honestly say that any wish I have had about my life has come true

Jenny Girl *out on the bay.*

23

REGRETS & BLESSINGS

Twenty years from now you will be more disappointed by the things
that you didn't do than by the ones you did do.
So throw off the bowlines. Sail away from the safe harbor.
Catch the trade winds in your sails. Explore. Dream. Discover.

~ Mark Twain

When I made the decision to write this book, I admit I didn't know the first thing about how to go about doing it. I'll bet I started the first chapter forty, maybe even fifty different times over the course of several months. I had so many thoughts that I wanted to stress, so many ideas that I believed had the chance to be inspirational to someone. I didn't want the book to be just a diary of the torment and demons I was forced to wrestle, I wanted it to be a guide for sufferers so *they could compare and contrast my experiences with their own thoughts and feelings. There is tremendous value in that.*

So where should I begin? Maybe, I thought, I would have better luck beginning with the end. Therefore, what follows below is the beginning I wrote for this book, which as we have now come full circle, is the ending.

~Brian

The Cape Cod beach where I worked on much of this book.

Today, I am sitting on a beach on Cape Cod. It's one of my favorite places in the world to be. It's 5:30 on a Thursday evening, and my family is due to arrive tomorrow.

If there ever was a perfect night to start to write a book, I think this would have to be it. I have decided to start with the last page of the book and try to work through my story backwards. I have read hundreds of books in my lifetime, but unlike some people I know, I won't skip to the end to find out who died or who the murderer is. It ruins the whole book! And biographies and history are no different -- even though you generally know the outcome, you still don't know how that person feels about things now. It's as if people think they get some strange advantage by skipping 200 pages of fluff just because they are dying to know the answer at the end. For me though, it's all about the journey. It is therapy.

I think starting from the end will make it easier to jog my memory. Much of I want to discuss in this book is extremely emotional, personal and sensitive, including many things I wish I could simply forget ever happened. I expect I will be redundant, I will mimic, and I am going to repeat myself, but one thing I promise never to do is exaggerate. As I sit here on the calmest beach on the planet, I can feel myself becoming anxious because I know that in the coming months, I will need to relive past moments and memories that caused me so much pain. And I expect to discover that even the most painful pieces I don't remember now are still there, rooted somewhere in the recesses of my subconscious. It's sort of like unpacking a drawer full of old sweaters. By the time you remove a few of them off the top you discover a bunch more underneath you totally forgot you owned.

Well, I plan to introduce you to many of those old sweaters. And hopefully I will be able to use them to tell a story that sufferers of severe panic and anxiety will be able to relate to. Looking back at all the customers I've known, the vendors I've met, and the hundreds of trips I've taken, I literally shake my head in amazement at the financial goals and successes I've been able to attain while dealing with this terrible condition. I would never have dreamed 30 years ago that I would be here at this point in my life and be able to help people by talking about something that humiliated me for so long. I've been to New York, Maryland, New Jersey, North Carolina, Florida, Toronto, Chicago and so many other places more times than I can count, all the while battling with these demons, taking them along for the ride.

I am already finding this difficult. Tears are filling my eyes. I'm not embarrassed to say I take pride in what I've accomplished in my career. At the workshops I deliver back at my Motivate for Success facility, I teach the lessons I plan to talk about in this book.

One of the messages I try to deliver is that success is not perfection -- merely a little above average. I consider myself an average person in just about every way imaginable. I don't have the athletic ability of a pro, nor the looks of Sylvester Stallone, or even the education of most -- which is mostly my own doing. We're all created imperfect. And what I do have, more than most people, is insecurity even though I come across as strong and confident. Later in the book, I will talk about this technique which is called "act as if" that will be an integral part of a toolbox that you will read all about and that you can use to work through your own problems.

My business partner was only the latest of about twenty people who said that I have to write this all down. They think it's an extraordinary story. And now, I've reached that point in my life where I think I'm ready. I have never been the kind of guy who pats himself on the back every time something goes right in his life. And if one day we meet and you get to know me, you'll realize that. I believe it's part of what has held me back from writing this until now. For the greater part of my life, I couldn't admit it. But I want you to understand the extraordinary things you can truly do.

I consider myself blessed and I am grateful for everything in my life. I have travelled over highways and byways, through the air thousands of miles to build my business, living every moment in fear and terror. I have spent countless nights crying alone in my room, or hunched over the steering wheel in my car, covered by a shroud of anxiety and self-doubt. All because I was panic-stricken and I could not show my fear. You'll read all about it. In many ways, I wish I was already finished writing it.

Sometimes I get pissed off because people see what I have and they don't understand what I went through to get it. There's a part of me that says, "Who gives a shit what they think." Then another part of me wants to tell them -- why don't you go and deal with all the shit I've been through, travel all the miles in terror that I've travelled, deal with the emotional torture and demons for years, be rejected hundreds and hundreds of times, be utterly afraid to leave your own home, leave a company that went out of business to start your own company from nothing, and then when you are done with all that -- stand on a mountaintop and tell everyone about it. Go ahead and tell the world everything you've lived through, your feelings, your doubts, your emotional wounds... and if you want to do that for 35 years and survive, then God bless you.

I do have regrets, however. My greatest regret is that I have never told my wife half the things I plan to write about in this book. I regret that she's going to learn things as she reads this, and will feel terrible that she didn't know. It's not my intent to hurt her or anyone else. I regret the fact that my mother and father didn't know what I was going through, either. The torment was terrible and I didn't wish to share it with anyone. And I regret the fact that I did not write this book sooner because I might have been able to help so many more people.

I am blessed.

But right now, I feel grateful and blessed. I'm on a wonderful beach waiting for my family with security in the bank, a smile on my face, and a joy in my heart. And if this was God's way of using me to tell my story and help people, then I have no choice but to be grateful. Next week I will really get into the core of writing this book and hopefully I'll be happy with the final product. I am a little anxious and scared to actually get started, to be honest, but at this moment I am thirsty as hell... so I will now leave the beach and go back to the house for a drink and play a little country music as I watch the sunset.

And for those of you who like to skip to the last chapter, let me save you the trouble and tell you right up front how this book will end -- Life is good.

ACKNOWLEDGEMENTS

It was a close friend and business associate who looked at me across dinner in a local restaurant after one of my motivational workshops and said, "*Brian... you have to write this fucking book!*"

As I drove home that night, I tried to figure out exactly what kind of book it was that I wanted to write. My wife also encouraged me to do it, and as she would learn, I had lived through many emotional and embarrassing moments she didn't know about. There were several chapters I asked her to review to confirm details, facts, dates, and times. I watched her read them in front of me and couldn't help but see the hurt and pain reflected back in her eyes. No one knows me better than she does, and still she didn't know about any of this. I told her no -- I wouldn't write it, but she insisted. She knew I had to do it. She knew the number of people that it could potentially help.

My co-author, Steve Porter, said that in this type of memoir, you want to try to limit your words and stay focused on the story you are trying to tell. I didn't realize how hard that was to do. Imagine the experiences from over thirty years of stories from childhood, high school, my years in business, the gym and all that goes with that? I had 150 friends at my bachelor party alone and none of them knew -- they were all my friends and buddies -- and

I could tell a story about each one of them. I once went to England with a band, worked as a bouncer in a bar, and took some wild trips to Ft. Lauderdale. But the best time of my life was getting married and starting a family -- it grounded me. It also drove me to want to get better and heal. Now I'm not sure it would have been possible to put all those feelings, emotions, and experiences accumulated over forty years into words. If I had, this book would be 5,000 pages long.

The biggest challenge was telling my story and sharing the tools that are relevant and relate to your own anxieties and fears. I've pinpointed and shared specific examples and circumstances from my life to illustrate that, but please note that there were many more instances I could have written about and that I continue to discuss in my workshops. One point I want to make here is that despite the horrors, the good has far exceeded the bad. I now enjoy my life tremendously. I accept that I have always had agoraphobia, but I've dealt with it and learned to let it go.

We travel together as a family many times a year. We are fortunate. I am also fortunate to have time to ski, boat, and take motorcycle rides all by myself. The testing is over and the living has started. I wouldn't trade my experiences for anything in the world even though it was an ordeal. But I am now on a new path, and this path has helped me appreciate even more the joy my family brings me. I am blessed to have a heart and mind full of happiness.

May you live all the days of your life.

AFTERWORD

by Steven R. Porter

Fear is a complex and powerful emotion that carries with it an astonishing range of effects and influence. Fear has the power to keep you off a roller coaster, and the clout to stop you from asking someone out on a date. Fear might convince you to stay quiet and not rise to share your thoughts in front of an audience, or it could keep you from ever setting foot in your spider-infested tool shed ever again.

And as we saw on 9/11, in the hands of the profoundly desperate and evil, fear can be wielded as a weapon more powerful than an army and can disrupt nations in a moment, control millions and change the world as we know it, forever.

From this assessment many would infer that fear is a great evil, a danger, a weakness and something we must avoid at any cost – *fearing fear itself*, so to speak. But do our customary reactions to true fear possess a deeper meaning? It is quite possible that this essential element of human existence requires not avoidance but instead our constant attention, respect and understanding to control it.

Fear is the most primitive of human emotions, and has an intimate tie to the other so-called negative emotions like sadness, fright, dread, anxiety and anger. Its origins are no doubt rooted at the beginning of human evolution when survival of our kind was not assured; and perhaps competing species that did not possess this important ability to be "afraid" were summarily consumed, destined to fall into the anonymity of permanent extinction. Fear is normal. Fear keeps us safe. Fear remains a prime motivator in our quest for survival.

As a novelist, I often find myself pondering the motives of the characters I create. I give them obstacles, and I wonder if their actions are consistent with their feelings as they battle through them. Are they believable? It haunts me. Would I myself do such a thing? Entire genres of writing have emerged out of the motivations of love (romance) and curiosity (mystery). Yet oddly, within the genre of fear (horror), books and stories are more commonly written not necessarily to explain the actions of characters, but instead, are written to scare the bejeezus out of the reader. It turns out that fear is also fun when controlled, and can even be exhilarating when defeated.

It was for this reason I was both honored and excited to be invited to work with Brian and help him tell his extraordinary story. Characters in novels and movies are left with neatly-packaged black and white choices -- overcome their fears or surrender to them. Rocky could have walked away from that fight with Apollo Creed that he knew he couldn't win -- yet he stepped into the ring choosing to fight anyway. The story of how Brian faced his fears and overcame them provides important insight for us all. Whether inflicted with an anxiety disorder or not, the tools described in this book can be applied to anyone who sees anxiety as an obstacle to their own happiness.

But Brian is no fictional character, and the choice he made not to succumb to fear but instead to accept it and overcome it – *to do it anyway* – was far from a simple one. This is real life and Brian is real flesh and blood existing in the real world and in real time. And Brian is also quick to point out that there is a huge difference between real fear like the fear of terrorism and the imagined fear that he has suffered and battled for decades. Yet it is harder to make such a simple separation of the physical and emotional reactions within the human mind. The experience and feelings remain eerily the same.

As children, we believe that the monster under our beds will eat us – an extraordinary and necessary creation of the human imagination. The prospect of such a monster terrifies us – our heart rate rises, we sweat, we hyperventilate, we cry. As adults, we giggle at the thought, yet that monster, though imagined, is as real and horrific as anything we've experienced to that point in our young, restricted world. That monster is important and teaching our young selves lessons about fear, fearing the unknown and the eventual realization that some kinds of fear are imaginary after all -- no child to date has ever been eaten by that monster. It's an important experience we all live through before we are faced with tangible fears later in life. It's how we safely develop important personal traits like courage, bravery, strength and understanding. It's terror with training wheels. We are born with the innate ability to know that the world we aspire to live in is a very dangerous and scary place.

Brian and I are listed here as co-authors, but the anecdotes, stories, experiences, moments and lessons chronicled in this book are all authentically Brian's. My role in the creation of this book was to be the incubator -- a surrogate -- to help direct, shape and craft the narrative in such a way that these true, unbelievable moments are believable. It was Brian's belief that if his story could be told with truth, authenticity and compassion, many who allow fear and panic to rule their lives will be helped. It is my hope we have achieved that lofty goal, and perhaps even more.

ABOUT THE AUTHORS

Brian Beneduce is the owner and founder of Ocean State Packaging, a multi-million dollar international plastics packaging supplier based in East Greenwich, Rhode Island that provides high quality and complete plastics packaging solutions to a variety of industries. In 2001, Brian founded "Motivate for Success" to share his story, and through it, offer motivational seminars and presentations to individuals and groups all over the country, helping people overcome their own anxiety and fears. Brian and his wife Robbie have two children and currently live in Rhode Island.

Steven R. Porter is a publisher and writer, as well as the author of two independently published novels -- the crime thriller *Confessions of the Meek & the Valiant* and the award-winning historical novel *Manisses* based on the history and legends of Block Island. He is the founder and president of the Association of Rhode Island Authors which has grown in just four years to include over 270 members. He and his wife Dawn live in Glocester, Rhode Island where they own and operate Stillwater River Publications.

Advance Praise for

Scared to Death... Do It Anyway

For those suffering with severe anxiety and panic, this book will offer the "yes, that's my life!" sense that books written by clinicians just can't quite capture. Brian does an excellent job expressing just how awful true severe anxiety feels — physically, emotionally, and mentally — and how isolating it can be. He goes beyond the clinical symptom checklist that anyone can read online to offer countless examples of how severe anxiety colors the lenses through which sufferers see the world, leading to interpretations and automatic thoughts that intrude, dictate, and debilitate. Brian also shows us that sometimes people who are still functioning day-to-day may be truly suffering on the inside.

"Scared to Death... Do It Anyway" is a valuable resource for loved ones of those suffering from severe anxiety and panic, as well. While many people can empathize with feeling nervous, overly worried, and "busy-brained," it is really hard for family and friends to imagine all the barriers and reasons why those suffering can't just "face it," or "stop worrying so much." It is my hope that those who are living the kind of anxiety-ridden life that Brian describes will read this resource and be motivated by the realty that they **can** be less anxious and happier, through learning what is happening in the body, how thinking can be destructive, and that there are tools to challenge and tolerate severe anxiety in healthy ways. This is a great companion for the guided work of cognitive-behavioral therapy!

Jessica L. Stewart, Psy.D.
Clinical & School Psychologist
Providence, Rhode Island

Made in the USA
Charleston, SC
23 February 2016